Vicarius Christi

The Vicar of Christ

Michele Doucette, M.Ed.

Vicarius Christi: The Vicar of Christ

Copyright © 2012 by Michele Doucette, St. Clair Publications

All rights reserved. No part of this publication may be reproduced or transmitted in any form or by any means, electronic or mechanical, including photocopying, recording, or by any information storage and retrieval system, without written permission from the author.

ISBN 978-1-935786-37-5

Printed in the United States of America by

St. Clair Publications

PO Box 726

McMinnville, TN   37111-0726

http://stclairpublications.com/

Table of Contents

Dedication 1

Author's Note 3

Historical Background... 7

Church Kingship.. 15

The Elven Peoples... 25

The Cathars and the Knights Templar 32

Historical Fact 47

What Does This Mean?.. 56

Doom and Gloom Hype 66

Context for Today 124

Bibliography... 135

About the Author 167

Dedication

This book is dedicated to a dear family friend John Delaney (known as JW, Da Lin and extended family member) of the past twenty-six years, who transitioned on November 26, 2011 in Xuzhou, China.

Life is but a journey to one's self. We are here to discover that we need not seek anything outside of our own Being. Some might prefer to call this a rediscovery of the true self.

The ability to express forgiveness, allowing others the outcome of their own experience(s), without changing the nature of who you truly are, is the mastery to which all can attain, for therein lies the healing of all illusion, all separation, all duality.

Truly this is also an important and essential part of what we have come here to experience.

As spoken by the Dalai Lama, *the highest happiness is when one reaches the stage of liberation, at which there is no more suffering.*

Vicarius Christi: The Vicar of Christ

While we shall miss the special telephone calls from China, I am sure this deeply philosophical soul is now bantering with the likes of Aristotle himself.

Author's Note

In the noteworthy words of Pierre Teilhard de Chardin, a French philosopher and Jesuit priest, who trained as both a paleontologist as well as a geologist, as penned in his 1955 publication, Le Phénomène Humain [1] ...

We are not human beings having a spiritual experience; we are spiritual beings having a human experience.

In essence, this means that we are not human beings on a spiritual journey. Rather, we are spiritual beings on a journey into what it means to be human.

So, too, were these his words from the same publication ...

A universal love is not only psychologically possible; it is the only complete and final way in which we are able to love.

---

[1] http://www.archive.org/details/phenomenon-of-man-pierre-teilhard-de-chardin.pdf

Vicarius Christi: The Vicar of Christ

Julian Huxley, in his introduction to <u>The Phenomena of Man</u> (1955), wrote: "It can be said that he applied his whole life, his tremendous intellect and his great spiritual faith to the concept of building up a philosophy that would reconcile Christian theology with the scientific theory of evolution, that would relate the facts of religious experience to those of natural science. <u>The Phenomenon of Man</u> is Pierre Teilhard's most important book and contains the quintessence of his thought. Its subject could be described as the surging evolution of the world, from the primal stuff of the universe, through life, to consciousness and man." [2]

Other Texts by Teilhard de Chardin [3]

The Human Phenomenon [4]

---

[2] http://en.wikiquote.org/wiki/Pierre_Teilhard_de_Chardin

[3] http://www.archive.org/search.php?query=creator%3A%22PIERRE+TEILHARD+DE+CHARDIN%22

[4] http://web.archive.org/web/20080506215945/http://www.webcom.com/gaia/tdc.html

Vicarius Christi: The Vicar of Christ

This volume, a slight departure from most of my written works, is wholeheartedly dedicated to those who are *not afraid* to challenge the status quo of long held personal belief systems. As a result, these same individuals usually find themselves engaged in an earnest search of their own inner truth(s); such is the nature of why we are here.

In the words of Andrew Cohen, editor of EnlightenNext magazine … *The awakening of the spiritual impulse in the human heart and mind is the universe becoming conscious of itself through its own emerging creative process. When you, an awakening human being, experience that urge, the intensity of your creative inspiration is coming from the First Cause itself. The interior of the cosmos is awakening to itself within you, and responding to its own highest aspiration, which is to become more conscious.*

We elected to come here to experience ourselves in all ways, to become more conscious, and to evolve from a spiritual standpoint.

To do so, we must embrace change.

Vicarius Christi: The Vicar of Christ

Andrew Cohen also shares that ... *Many people are scared of change, of that which is new. They are deeply attached to the status quo in which everything appears to be predictable, comfortable, and therefore, safe. But for what I call the evolutionary impulse – the energy and intelligence that gave rise to the universe and is animating our bodies, minds, and personalities in this very moment – that is a description of spiritual stagnation.*

When you awaken to the dynamism of that creative impulse in yourself, the only place you will feel truly comfortable is at the very edge of the leading edge; where, in every moment, everything is possible and new potentials continually emerge. Evolutionary Enlightenment is a spiritual path and practice that allows you to live on that edge; it creates the conditions within yourself for something new to emerge that has never existed before.

It is my utmost yearning that these words, cited herein, will become the reality of the greater multitude.

Historical Background

The Vicar of Christ, or *Vicarius Christi*, is a term, in keeping with the Papacy, that generally refers to the earthly representative of God or Christ; a most specific term (first appearing in the 5th century) used in reference to the Bishop of Rome (also known as the Pope). [5]

In metaphysical terms, can all, in reference to the term Christ Consciousness, aspire to becoming a Vicar of Christ? It is my belief that this is the *end goal for each of us*; one based on both enlightenment and transcendence.

Interestingly, *Vicarius Filii Dei*, meaning Vicar of the Son of God, as in a physical representative, is a phrase that was first used in the medieval Donation of Constantine to refer to Saint Peter, a leader of the Early Christian Church who was regarded as the first Pope by the Catholic Church. [6][7][8]

---

[5] http://en.wikipedia.org/wiki/Vicar_of_Christ
[6] http://en.wikipedia.org/wiki/Vicarius_Filii_Dei
[7] http://en.wikipedia.org/wiki/Donation_of_Constantine
[8] http://en.wikipedia.org/wiki/Constantine_I

Vicarius Christi: The Vicar of Christ

In truth, this *forged* document was an imperial decree by which the Byzantine Emperor Constantine I *supposedly* transferred authority, over Rome and the western part of the Roman Empire, to the Pope.

Constantine founded the City of Constantinople in 324 AD and yet the document *was said to have been* signed in 315 AD.

Who was it that forged the document, you ask? Why, the Papal chancery, of course.

Fraudulently proclaimed to be the Vicar of Christ, this concocted document set forth a new precedent: the local bishop of Rome (aka the Pope) could now sanction *who* became king.

In 496 AD, Clovis I was the Merovingian king.[9] It is said that he was of a special bloodline going back to Yeshua (Jesus), meaning the House of David.

---

[9] 45th G grandfather of the author

Vicarius Christi: The Vicar of Christ

In 496 AD, the Roman Church was *not* the dominant establishment, meaning that it was in competition with other groups (such as Arianism, for example).

It was King Clovis who, following his own conversion, was responsible for persuading much of Western Europe to convert to Christianity, thereby "firmly establishing Catholicism as the dominant religion within the Merovingian Kingdom, and saving the Church from almost certain collapse." [10]

The Church "agreed to pledge their allegiance to Clovis and promised that a new Holy Empire would be established under the auspices of the Merovingians." [11]

In return for Clovis having been proclaimed *Novus Constantinus* (emperor of a to-be-created Holy Roman Empire; a title which referenced the *New Constantine*), he agreed to make use of his armies to crush any denominations that were in direct competition with the Roman Church.

---

[10] http://www.juneaustin.co.uk/merovingians.html
[11] Ibid.

Vicarius Christi: The Vicar of Christ

When they granted him this title, Clovis "had no reason to doubt the sincerity of the Church, but unbeknownst to him, he had unwittingly become a pawn in a conspiracy for the Church to eventually seize control of his Kingdom, thereby establishing the Pope as the supreme ruler." [12]

We are now going to fast forward to Dagobert II, son of Sigebert, grandson of Lothar and great grandson of Clovis I, also of the Merovingian line, born in 651 AD. It is said that because he was lax in serving the wishes of the Roman Church, thereby incurring "ecclesiastical displeasure," he was assassinated on December 23, 679 AD. [13] [14]

The successive Mayors of the Palace, namely, [1] Pépin II (c. 635 to 714; the first Duke of the Franks and father of Charles Martel, illegitimate son through his mistress, Alpaida), [2] Charles Martel (c. 686 to 741; grandfather of Charlemagne) and [3] Pépin III, also called Pépin the Short (c. 714 to 768; father of Charlemagne), continued to gain in personal power.

---

[12] http://www.juneaustin.co.uk/merovingians.html
[13] http://doubleuoglobe.com/vol11/cn11-79.html
[14] http://www.juneaustin.co.uk/merovingians.html

Vicarius Christi: The Vicar of Christ

Pépin III was not satisfied with being Mayor; he wanted more. He wanted to be king.

Coming to an arrangement with the Pope, by virtue of the spuriously forged document, none other than the <u>Donation of Constantine</u> (mysteriously discovered in 751 AD and supposedly written some 400 years earlier), he was proclaimed king, leading to the removal, and imprisonment, of the true Merovingian king, Childeric III. [15] [16] [17] [18] [19]

As a means of legitimizing a claim, as was generally the case with royalty, it must also be shared that the maternal great grandmother of Charlemagne was Bertrada of Prüm, a Merovingian princess.

It is thought that she was the daughter of Merovingian king Theuderic III (son of Clovis II and Bathilde) and Clotilde of Heristal.

---

[15] http://en.wikipedia.org/wiki/Pepin_II_the_Middle
[16] http://en.wikipedia.org/wiki/Charles_Martel
[17] http://en.wikipedia.org/wiki/Pepin_the_Short
[18] http://doubleuoglobe.com/vol11/cn11-79.html
[19] http://en.wikipedia.org/wiki/Childeric_III

Vicarius Christi: The Vicar of Christ

Childeric I [20]

Franks and Holy Romans [21]

Franks: Merovingian Kings [22]

International World History Project [23]

Kinship and Y-Chromosome Analysis of 7th Century Human Remains [24]

Library of Halexandria: Dark Ages and Merovingians [25]

List of Frankish Kings [26]

Merovingian Dynasty [27]

---

[20] http://en.wikipedia.org/wiki/Childeric_I
[21] http://www.mmdtkw.org/MedRomUnit0600-0PixList.html
[22] http://fmg.ac/Projects/MedLands/MEROVINGIANS.htm
[23] http://history-world.org/mainmenu.htm
[24] http://www.ncbi.nlm.nih.gov/pmc/articles/PMC2702742/pdf/CroatMedJ_50_0286.pdf
[25] http://www.halexandria.org/dward216.htm
[26] http://en.wikipedia.org/wiki/List_of_Frankish_kings
[27] http://en.wikipedia.org/wiki/Merovingian_dynasty

Vicarius Christi: The Vicar of Christ

Mythology of Bees [28]

Royal Museums of Art and History: Merovingians [29]

St. Clair Research: Ergolding, Germany – Archaeology Meets FTDNA [30]

St. Clair Research: Sinclair DNA Maybe Not Merovingian DNA [31]

The Bees of Napoleon [32]

The Bee, Part 1 [33]

The Bee, Part 2 [34]

The Bee, Part 3 [35]

---

[28] http://lunedemiel.tm.fr/anglais/06.htm
[29] http://www.kmkg-mrah.be/merovingians
[30] http://www.stclairresearch.com/content/ergolding.html
[31] http://www.stclairresearch.com/content/Sinclair-DNA-Merovingian.html
[32] http://regencyredingote.wordpress.com/2010/10/22/the-bees-of-napoleon/
[33] http://www.andrewgough.co.uk/bee1_1.html
[34] http://www.andrewgough.co.uk/bee2_1.html
[35] http://www.andrewgough.co.uk/bee3_1.html

Vicarius Christi: The Vicar of Christ

The G2a Skeleton from Ergolding, Bavaria [36]

The Merovingian House [37]

The Merovingians [38]

The Merovingians (Robert Sewell) [39]

Tomb of Childeric [40] [41] [42] [43]

Who Were These G2a's? [44]

---

[36] http://dna-forums.org/index.php?/topic/12940-the-g2a-viicentury-skeleton-from-ergoldingbavaria/page__st__20
[37] http://allfaith.com/prophecy/merovingian.html
[38] http://www.bibliotecapleyades.net/esp_merovingios.htm#menu
[39] http://www.robertsewell.ca/merovech.html
[40] http://www.andrewgough.co.uk/forum/viewtopic.php?f=35&t=3027
[41] http://archaeology.about.com/od/tterms/g/tournai.htm
[42] http://www.findagrave.com/cgi-bin/fg.cgi?page=gr&GRid=63938162
[43] http://history.furman.edu/webimages/index.htm
[44] http://listsearches.rootsweb.com/th/read/Y-DNA-HAPLOGROUP-G/2009-06/1243873954

Church Kingship

As denoted by eminent chroniclers such as Hegesippus, Africanus and Eusebius, it was during the 1st century that the Messianic heirs (meaning the descendants of Yeshua and his family) were hunted down and put to the sword by Roman Emperors; once the Roman Church was operative by the 4th century, the dynasty was forever doomed. [45]

The imperative question, then, becomes: *why* would the early Roman Church have dedicated itself to eradicating the descendants of Yeshua (Jesus) and his family?

In retrospect, the Roman Church later directed specific brutal assaults (as in the Albigensian Crusades which began in 1209) and Catholic Inquisitions against all upholders and champions of the original concept of Grail kingship. [46]

---

[45] http://www.abovetopsecret.com/forum/thread138328/pg1
[46] Ibid.

Vicarius Christi: The Vicar of Christ

Once again, one has to ask the pertinent question: *why* would the established Roman Church have dedicated itself to annihilating these cited populations?

Once again, we are back to the local bishop of Rome (aka the Pope) sanctioning *who* would become king.

Church kingship is a term that applies to all monarchs who have achieved their regnal positions by way of Church coronation (through either the Pope or another Christian leader, such as the Archbishop of Canterbury in Britain), prevailing from the 8th century onward. [47]

Previously, however, there was never any necessity for coronation because inheritance was always associated with a specific bloodline.

With the Papacy having usurped this power, under strict terms of sovereign practice, can it not be said, then, that all such monarchies and their affiliated governments are invalid?

---

[47] http://www.abovetopsecret.com/forum/thread138328/pg1

Vicarius Christi: The Vicar of Christ

To think all of this was made possible, courtesy of the *forged* medieval Donation of Constantine.

The provisions of this so-called document were then "enacted by the Vatican, whereupon the Merovingian Kings of the Grail bloodline in Gaul were deposed and a whole new puppet-dynasty was supplemented by way of a family of hitherto mayors. They were dubbed Carolingians and their only king of any significance was the legendary Charlemagne. By way of this strategy, the whole nature of monarchy changed from being an office of community guardianship to one of absolute rule and, by virtue of this monumental change, the long-standing code of princely service was forsaken as European kings became servants of the Church instead of being servants of the people." [48]

The Merovingians, thought to be descended from a tribe of Germanic people known as the Sicambrian Franks, are said to have claimed descent, both from Noah as well as from Troy. [49] Referred to as the long haired sorcerer kings, it is

---

[48] http://www.abovetopsecret.com/forum/thread138328/pg1
[49] http://www.juneaustin.co.uk/merovingians.html

said that they were "able to heal by the laying on of hands, and communicate clairvoyantly and telepathically with animals. It is rumoured that they each carried a distinctive birthmark in the form of a red cross either over the heart, or between the shoulder blades. Their powers were said to emanate from their long hair and extended to everything they possessed, even down to the tassels on their robes." [50]

They did not reign "by coronation, but rather by tradition, automatically assuming the rite of succession when they reached their twelfth birthday. In this respect, the day to day Government and administration were placed in the hands of the Chancellors, or Mayors of the Palace, ultimately leaving them wide open to manipulation. It was this that eventually led to their downfall." [51]

Despite the efforts of both Church and Pépin III, the Merovingian bloodline was *not* exterminated.

---

[50] http://www.juneaustin.co.uk/merovingians.html
[51] Ibid.

In time, this line "came to include Godfroi de Bouillon, founder of the Knights Templar." [52]

Whilst the Merovingians [53] had formerly "assumed the role of overseers, sages and wise counsellors, the Carolingians and their successors, prompted by the Church, became deliberately poorly educated, ignorant, insensitive tyrants and territorial tradesmen." [54]

The Grail Code "had died [only] to be replaced by a corrupted form of feudal totalitarianism and brutal, economic slavery as the Church carefully and strategically replaced the old dynasties with its own merchant-class client families who, from that day on, became vassals of the Vatican." [55]

In reality, "the Church, under the auspices of the Donation of Constantine was the sole and supreme temporal power in Europe and the known world. Without this purported

---

[52] http://www.juneaustin.co.uk/merovingians.html
[53] http://en.wikipedia.org/wiki/Merovingians
[54] http://herebedragons.weebly.com/constantine.html
[55] Ibid.

imperial benefice however, the Church would have remained a marginalized Mediterranean cult contesting for patronage along with a host of other gnostic Christian denominations."[56]

What this essentially means is that "no monarch reigning today, and no government under the monarch or instituted in their name, would enjoy their position if the Church, empowered by the <u>Donation</u>, had not given them permission to rule in the first place."[57]

Knowing, however, that the <u>Donation of Constantine</u> is a fraud, "the Church was *never* given any temporal powers at all, let alone the right to found dynasties, crown kings or institute government; the whole document was a lie from beginning to end and has been known to be a fake since Lorenzo Valla applied the methods of historical criticism to it during the Renaissance."[58]

---

[56] http://herebedragons.weebly.com/constantine.html
[57] Ibid.
[58] Ibid.

Vicarius Christi: The Vicar of Christ

We *know* that Valla was correct, mainly because "the New Testament references incorporated into the wording of the Donation were taken from the Latin Vulgate version of the Bible ... a Bible [that] was compiled by St. Jerome who was born more than two decades after Constantine was supposed to have signed the Donation ... [meaning that] the actual Vulgate Bible wording that appears in the Donation didn't exist until St Jerome invented it, fifty years after the document had supposedly been dated and signed by the Emperor. By this time, Constantine had been dead for decades." [59]

For further comparative purposes, "the language of the Donation is eighth century clerical or dog Latin, whilst the Latin used in the 4th century Empire was late classical Roman. The Imperial and Papal ceremonials described in the Donation didn't exist in Constantine's time, but were developed some centuries later." [60]

---

[59] http://herebedragons.weebly.com/constantine.html
[60] Ibid.

Vicarius Christi: The Vicar of Christ

Courtesy of the <u>Donation</u>, we understand "that Constantine offered the Pope all the robes and Crowns of office, but the Pope, being such a humble man, gave them back to the Emperor. This lets the Church off the hook should some malcontent turn up and ask for sartorial evidence … [further demonstrating] the pretentious egotism, the arrogance and the sheer material greed of the Church, as authors of the document." [61]

Given what we know about the <u>Donation</u>, in retrospect, "Britain has had no legally reigning monarch for 900 years; [a consequence that means that] all the laws passed by these monarchs were, and are, illegal and worthless, and all the governmental agencies set up by, or derived from, these monarchs or their laws are also illegal and worthless up to the present day." [62]

In continuation, "the reader might like to consider the fact that all the arrests ever made by the police in Britain and Europe are acts of kidnap and habeas corpus. Equally, any

---

[61] http://herebedragons.weebly.com/constantine.html
[62] Ibid.

man who has taken up arms for the Crown and killed for his country is unprotected by law and guilty, therefore, of murder." [63]

Knowing that "the entire British legal system is illegal, there are no laws, and so the crimes of habeas corpus and murder as we define them today, simply do not exist," [64] as paradoxical as that may seem.

It appears, therefore, that the "entire moral basis of our society is founded upon a massive historical lie which has twisted the minds of generations of individuals until they have become terrified of the natural drives of their own bodies and souls. The resultant taboos that have been created have been used to divide the minds of the people and make them dependant on the Church-State for solutions to the problems of resisting Satan and fighting temptation and sin, when these contrived, nonsensical, whimsies never existed in the first place." [65]

---

[63] http://herebedragons.weebly.com/constantine.html
[64] Ibid.
[65] Ibid.

Vicarius Christi: The Vicar of Christ

As is also reminiscent of the writings of David Icke, with his problem, reaction, solution [66] equation, the Church "created the confusion and the division and then offered the solution. In fear, the population invested its trust in the perfidious Church, and, in return for their confidence, the Church turned the people into slaves and an entire civilization into a manufacturing plant to service their own greed for luxury and power." [67]

---

[66] http://www.davidicke.com/headlines/46405-david-icke-problem-reaction-solution-explained
[67] http://herebedragons.weebly.com/constantine.html

The Elven Peoples

In the Cathar language of old Provence, "a female elf was an albi (elbe or ylbi), and Albi was the name given to the main Cathar centre in Languedoc; this was in deference to the matrilinear heritage of the Grail dynasty, for the Cathars were supporters of the original *Albi*-gens: the Elven Bloodline which had descended through the Dragon Queens of yore, such as Lilith, Miriam, Bathsheba and Mary Magdalene. It was for this reason that, when Simon de Montfort,[68] and the armies of Pope Innocent III, descended upon the region in 1209, it was called the Albigensian Crusade. Through some 35 years, tens of thousands of innocent people were slaughtered in this brutal campaign, all because the inhabitants of the region were champions of the original concept of Grail kingship, and against the pseudo-style of monarchy that had been implemented by the papal machine."[69]

---

[68] 26th G grandfather of the author
[69] http://watch.pair.com/michael-archangel.html

Vicarius Christi: The Vicar of Christ

It has been stated that the Roman Church oppressed the Elven peoples; namely, the Royal Scythian tribe [70] that "dwelled in the Black Sea Area and Asia Minor (the area around modern-day Romania, Ukraine, Turkey, and Iraq) and that the bloodlines of the *Grail* dynasties sprung from them via intermarriages between this tribe and Egyptian and Hebrew royalty in ancient times." [71]

Given their declared eastern origin, some scholars, before the 20th century, "assumed that the Scythians were descended from the Turkic (Mongolic) people. The Scythian community did inhabit western Mongolia in the 5th and 6th centuries, but were not Mongolian. The mummy of a Scythian warrior, which is believed to be about 2,500 years old, was a 30-to-40 year old man with blond hair, and was found in the Altai, Mongolia." [72] [73] [74]

---

[70] http://en.wikipedia.org/wiki/Scythian
[71] http://cyberalfheim.info/thousandyear.html
[72] http://www.ucg.org/booklet/united-states-and-britain-bible-prophecy/mysterious-scythians-burst-history/
[73] http://www.spiegel.de/international/0,1518,433600,00.html
[74] http://en.wikipedia.org/wiki/Scythians

Interestingly, red hair has also been found in Asia, most "notably among the Tocharians, who occupied the Tarim Basin in what is now the north western province of China. Many of the 2nd millennium BC Caucasian Tarim mummies in China have been found with red and blonde hair." [75] The earliest Egyptian pharaohs, it is said, "often had yellow or red hair, matching the Tocharian mummies." [76]

Mitochondrial DNA, extracted from "skeletal remains obtained from excavated Scythian kurgans, have produced a myriad of results and conclusions" in that the analysis "of the HV1 sequence obtained from a male Scytho-Siberian's remains at the Kizil site in the Altai Republic revealed the individual possessed the N1a maternal lineage. The study also noted that haplogroup mtDNA N1a was found at a relatively high frequency in the southern fringes of the Eurasian steppe, Iran (8.3%). From this, a possible link to ancient populations presumed to have come from Europe

---

[75] http://www.geni.com/projects/%E2%99%A5-Redheads
[76] Olsson, Suzanne. (2005) *Jesus in Kashmir: The Lost Tomb* (page 14). Charleston, SC:Booksurge.

that lived in the neighboring northwestern parts of the subcontinent, and Iran, was suggested." [77] [78] [79]

Additionally, mitochondrial DNA was also "extracted from two Scytho-Siberian skeletons found in the Altai Republic (Russia) dating back 2,500 years. Both remains were determined to be of males from a population who had characteristics of mixed Euro-Mongoloid origin. One of the individuals was found to carry the F2a maternal lineage, and the other the D lineage, both of which are characteristic of East Eurasian populations." [80]

The maternal genetic analysis "of the Saka period male and female skeletal remains from a double inhumation kurgan located at the Beral site in Kazakhstan determined that the two were most likely not closely related and were possibly husband and wife. The HV1 mitochondrial sequence of the male was similar to the Anderson sequence which is most frequent in European populations. Contrary, the HV1

---

[77] http://en.wikipedia.org/wiki/Kurgans
[78] http://www.spiegel.de/international/0,1518,433600,00.html
[79] http://en.wikipedia.org/wiki/Scythians
[80] Ibid.

sequence of the female suggested a greater likelihood of Asian origins. The study's findings were in line with the hypothesis that mixings between Scythians and other populations occurred. This was buttressed by the discovery of several objects with a Chinese inspiration in the grave. No conclusive associations with haplogroups were made, although it was suggested that the female may have derived from either mtDNA X or D." [81]

The haplotypes and haplogroups of 26 ancient human specimens "from the Krasnoyarsk area in Siberia dated from between the middle of the second millennium BC to the 4th century AD (Scythian and Sarmatian timeframe). Nearly all subjects belong to haplogroup R1a1-M17 which is thought to mark the eastward migration of the early Indo-Europeans. The results also confirm that throughout the Bronze and Iron Ages, south Siberia was a region of overwhelmingly predominant Europoid settlement, suggesting an eastward migration of Kurgan people across the Russo-Kazakh steppe. Finally, the study authors suggest that their data

---

[81] http://en.wikipedia.org/wiki/Scythians

shows that between Bronze and Iron Ages, the constellation of populations known variously as Scythians, Andronovians, etc., were blue (or green) eyed, fair-skinned and light-haired people which might have played a role in the early development of the Tarim Basin civilization." [82] [83]

This further confirms impressions "based on depictions of Scythian men in art. Scythians possessed pronounced Europoid faces and sported a beard and long hair; perhaps most resembling later medieval Slavs. This is confirmed by accounts of the Alans, a successor ancient Iranic steppe group, who were described by Ammianius as being tall and blonde." [84] [85]

4,000 Year Old Caucasian Mummies in Tarim Basin, Central Asia [86]

---

[82] http://en.wikipedia.org/wiki/Tarim_Basin
[83] http://en.wikipedia.org/wiki/Scythians
[84] http://en.wikipedia.org/wiki/Alans
[85] http://en.wikipedia.org/wiki/Scythians
[86] http://www.semp.us/publications/biot_reader.php?BiotID=665

Vicarius Christi: The Vicar of Christ

A Host of Mummies, A Forest of Secrets [87]

Evidence that a West-East admixed population lived in the Tarim Basin as early as the early Bronze Age [88]

Secrets of the Silk Road [89]

Tarim Mummies [90]

The Takla Makan Mummies [91]

When West Went East [92]

---

[87] http://www.nytimes.com/2010/03/16/science/16archeo.html
[88] http://www.biomedcentral.com/1741-7007/8/15/
[89] http://www.penn.museum/silkroad/home.php
[90] http://en.wikipedia.org/wiki/Tarim_mummies
[91] http://www.meshrep.com/PicOfDay/mummies/mummies.htm
[92] http://www.upenn.edu/gazette/0111/feature2_1.html

The Cathars and the Knights Templar

It was the 2003 release of Dan Brown's <u>The Da Vinci Code</u> that "sent the Catholic Church into a tizzy, because of claims that Yeshua ben Joseph (known nowadays as Jesus Christ) married Mary Magdalene and had children, siring the line of the Merovingian kings. Jesus was said to be of the House of David, and any descendants of His (if He had them) would have been of the Davidic (Desposynic) descent." [93]

Is it true? Did Jesus marry? Did he sire a bloodline of ancient kings?

Whatever you may believe about the Merovingians, "we are now coming to the part that can actually be historically verified without a doubt; there is no argument that the Roman Catholic Church systematically persecuted and disenfranchised every group said to be associated with the Grail Bloodline; the Merovingians, the Cathars, and the Knights Templar all suffered at the hands of the Roman

---

[93] http://cyberalfheim.info/thousandyear.html

Vicarius Christi: The Vicar of Christ

Pontiffs, who slandered them, tortured them, slaughtered them, and seized their lands in a series of coups, crusades, and inquisitions during the Middle Ages, such as the Albigensian Crusade from 1209 to 1229 AD, and the campaign of persecution that took place against the Templars in 1307 AD." [94]

The reason given "for the Church's campaign against the Cathars is generally that they were practitioners of a form of Gnostic Christianity," [95] a practice that was deemed heretical. During the early formation of what would later come to be known as Christianity, church authorities (deemed Fathers of the Church of Rome) exerted considerable influence (energy) in weeding out what they termed *false* doctrine.

The Cathars (stated to have been derived from the Greek word, *katharoi*, meaning pure ones), it is said, most emulated the Gnostics.

---

[94] http://cyberalfheim.info/thousandyear.html
[95] Ibid.

While the writings of the Cathars have, for the most part, been destroyed (because of the doctrinal threat as perceived by the Papacy), there are a few texts that were preserved by their opponents.

The *Rituel Cathare de Lyon* provides us with a mere glimpse of the inner working of their faith.

A Latin manuscript, *The Book of Two Principles*, kept in Florence, is "a translation made in 1260 from a work by the Cathar Jean de Lugio from Bergamo (written in 1230). The Latin translation, found in Prague in 1939, came from an anonymous treaty written in Languedoc at the beginning of the 13th century." [96] It is conceivable that the author may have been the Parfait Barthelemy of Carcassonne. This particular work outlines "the basis of a complete dualism that is reflected in a veiled way in the Holy Scriptures." [97]

---

[96] The Books by Gilles C. H.Nullens accessed on April 25, 2011 at http://www.nullens.org/catholics-heretics-and-heresy/part-1-the-cathars/1-2-introduction-to-the-cathar-religion-2/

[97] *Cathar Church and Doctrine* article accessed on April 25, 2011 at http://lespiraldelconeixement.com/dossier.cfm?lang=en&id=42

Vicarius Christi: The Vicar of Christ

In accordance with Cathari belief, Jesus came to transmit a message, to reveal the truth (as related to our *real* eternal and spiritual essence) and *not* to redeem the sins of all men by his death.

Likewise, the beliefs of the Cathars very much coincided with Jesus' example of life (through his teachings); namely, "non-violence but pure love, rejection of using the evil or force to resist the evil, and holy will in responding to attacks of evil only with sacrifice." [98]

Their message was one of love, tolerance, freedom and equality between men and women, and yet they were slaughtered by the Roman Church.

In medieval France, it was this sect of enlightened mystics that "tried to preserve Christ's true message," [99] possibly because they possessed "evidence of a more authentic version of early Christianity, much more dangerous than a

---

[98] *Cathar Church and Doctrine* article accessed on April 25, 2011 at http://lespiraldelconeixement.com/dossier.cfm?id=44
[99] http://www.ru.org/spirituality/remembering-the-cathars.html

Vicarius Christi: The Vicar of Christ

Jewish bloodline ... ancient scrolls containing lost teachings of Christ that contradicted the canonical gospels." [100]

In their own time, the Cathars were known as *Les Bons Hommes*, meaning *the good people*. "Their involvement with helping fight poverty and their denial of the authority of the church are important arguments for some researchers to place the Cathars firmly in the 12th century as church reformists and mystical Christians who reacted to the riches and despotism in the Roman Church." [101]

Despite the fact that St. Bernard of Clairvaux tried to bring the Cathars back into the orthodox fold of the church, it is worth citing his words ... *No sermons are more thoroughly Christian than theirs, and their morals are pure.* [102]

It was the very same St. Bernard of Clairvaux who was instrumental "in the planning, formation and promotion of the infant Templar Order," [103] and yet the "how and why St

---

[100] http://www.ru.org/spirituality/remembering-the-cathars.html
[101] http://www.et-in-arcadia-ego.com/html/Arcadia0B.php
[102] http://web.eecs.utk.edu/~mclennan/Classes/US310/Dante-Fedeli-d-Amore.html
[103] http://blog.templarhistory.com/2010/03/bernard-of-clairvaux/

Bernard became involved in the formation of the Knights Templar may never be fully understood. There is no doubt that he was blood-tied to some of the first Templar Knights, in particular André de Montbard, who was his maternal uncle. He may also have been related to the Counts of Champagne, who themselves appear to have been pivotal in the formation of the Templar Order." [104]

There exists a widespread belief that the Knights Templar and the Cathars had a similar world-view; a view that embraced a reverence of the Magdalene. It is also thought "that the Templars, who seem to have been great absorbers of other spiritualities from Sufism to Alchemy and Kabbalah, adopted certain key Cathar ideas." [105]

The Templars "swore their oath to both Bethany and the Magdalene, showing that their *inside knowledge* prevented them from blindly following the edicts of Rome." [106]

---

[104] http://blog.templarhistory.com/2010/03/bernard-of-clairvaux/
[105] http://templeofpegasus.blogspot.com/2008/09/enigma-of-cathars-epilogue.html
[106] Vayro, Ian Ross. (2007) *God Save Us From Religion* (page 187). Queensland, Australia: Joshua Books.

Vicarius Christi: The Vicar of Christ

It could well be that they knew about the early Hebrew traditions dating back "to the time of Solomon when there was not only Yahweh, but also the Goddess Ashtoreth, or Astarte (as she was known in Mesopotamia)." [107]

Astarte was also the counterpart of Ishtar, the Assyrian and Babylonian goddess. Mentioned several times in the Old Testament, this divine feminine being "was openly worshipped by the Israelites until the 6th century BC when she was replaced by the single supreme male god of Jehovah." [108]

The Cathars were known to have "referred to the Messianic dynasty from Jesus and Mary Magdalene as the *Albi*-gens; the Elven Bloodline." [109] In truth, the Albigensian Heresy was "melded around the Jewish Messianic Bloodline of Jesus that Rome so desperately sought to suppress, and this goes a long way towards explaining the Church's fanatical,

---

[107] http://www.laughingowl.com/aleta/Knightsandsecret.htm
[108] Ibid.
[109] Vayro, Ian Ross. (2007) *God Save Us From Religion* (page 188). Queensland, Australia: Joshua Books.

Vicarius Christi: The Vicar of Christ

unprecedented savagery against the peaceful and non-threatening Cathars." [110]

The Languedoc was a "major source of Templar income and recruits. The Templars partly owed their great expansion in the region to the support of the nobility with whom they were in close alliance, the combination of nobles' land and Templar capital allowing the establishment of new communities and the development of previously uncultivated territories. Some of these Templar patrons were renowned Cathar supporters." [111]

Templar castles, houses and fortresses, "were thick on the ground in Languedoc, the heartland of Catharism. They provided refuge for Perfects during the Albigensian Crusade. Many of the noble families of the area who supported Catharism also had Templar Knights in the family. Bertrand de Blanchefort, fourth Grand Master of the Templars, came from a Cathar family, and his descendants

---

[110] Vayro, Ian Ross. (2007) *God Save Us From Religion* (page 188). Queensland, Australia: Joshua Books.
[111] http://bogomiltocathar.devhub.com/blog/588653-templars-and-cathars/

fought with the Cathars against the Albigensian Crusaders." [112]

When the Templars "last stronghold in the Holy Land came under Muslim control, they established their headquarters in southern France, in the area now known as the Languedoc," [113] an area that was not officially part of France, given that it was "an independent principality ruled by a handful of noble families." [114]

The Languedoc "had much in common with Byzantium. They held knowledge and learning in high esteem" [115] and the nobility were both "literate and literary." [116]

Likewise, the Languedoc practiced "a civilized, easygoing religious tolerance, unlike the fanatical zeal that spread though most of Europe." [117]

---

[112] http://www.medievalmysteries.com/Templars.html
[113] http://www.laughingowl.com/aleta/Knightsandsecret.htm
[114] Ibid.
[115] Ibid.
[116] Ibid.
[117] Ibid.

Vicarius Christi: The Vicar of Christ

Catharism first appeared in southern France "sometime in the years following the First Crusade. Its adherents quickly became numerous and well organised, electing bishops, collecting funds and distributing money to the poor; but they could not accept that if there was only one God, and if God was the creator, and if God was good, that there should be suffering, illness and death in his world." [118]

The Cathars believed in "a good and an evil principle, the former the creator of the invisible and spiritual universe, the latter the creator of our material world. All matter was evil because it was the creation of the devil, but the ideal of renouncing the world was impractical for everyone, and so while most Cathars lived outwardly normal lives, pledging to renounce the evil world on their deathbeds, a few lived the strict life of the *perfecti*." [119]

The Cathars also believed in "reincarnation, the recognition of the feminine principle in religion, and that knowledge or *gnosis* took precedence over all creeds and dogma. They

---

[118] http://bogomiltocathar.devhub.com/blog/588653-templars-and-cathars/
[119] Ibid.

Vicarius Christi: The Vicar of Christ

formed their own church in opposition to Rome. They lived their lives in peace and harmony with nature. Women were held in high esteem, and allowed to preach." [120]

Word, of course, was sent to the Pope "that the Cathars were so inter-married into the local population of the region that it was impossible to identify who were Cathars and who weren't." [121] When asked how to discern the difference, the words uttered by Arnaud, the Cistercian abbott-commander, were *Caedite eos. Novit enim Dominus qui sunt eius.* [meaning *Kill them all. God will recognize his own*]. [122]

The traditional death toll, in a war against the Cathars, a peaceable Christian people, paragons of spirituality and virtue, has been cited as one million, as per the following sources: [1] John M. Robertson, <u>A Short History of Christianity</u> (London: Watts, 1902) p. 254; [2] Christopher Brookmyre, <u>Not the End of the World</u> (New York: Grove Press, 1998) p. 39; [3] Max Dimont, <u>Jews, God, and

---

[120] http://www.laughingowl.com/aleta/Knightsandsecret.htm
[121] Vayro, Ian Ross. (2007) *God Save Us From Religion* (page 188). Queensland, Australia: Joshua Books.
[122] http://en.wikipedia.org/wiki/Catharism

History (New York: Penguin, 1994) p. 225; [4] Dizerega Gus, Pagans & Christians: The Personal Spiritual Experience (St. Paul, MN: Llewellyn, 2001) p. 195; [5] Helen Ellerbe, The Dark Side of Christian History (Orlando, FL: Morningstar & Lark, 1995) p. 74, and [6] Michael Newton, Holy Homicide (Port Townsend, WA: Loompanics Unlimited, 1998) p. 117. [123]

Albigensian Crusade: Online Reference Book for Medieval Studies [124]

Andrew Gough's Arcadia [125]

Cathars and Cathar Beliefs in the Languedoc [126]

Cathars and Reincarnation [127]

---

[123] http://necrometrics.com/pre1700a.htm
[124] http://www.the-orb.net/textbooks/crusade/albig.html
[125] http://www.andrewgough.co.uk/
[126] http://www.cathar.info/
[127] http://www.innervision.com/mysteries/cathars.html

Vicarius Christi: The Vicar of Christ

Gordon Napier History Blog [128]

Legend of the Cathars [129]

Massacre at Montségur: A History of the Albigensian Crusade [130]

Montségur and The Cathars [131]

Primary Sources of the Albigensian Crusades [132]

Secrets of the Cathars [133]

The Albigensian Crusade [134]

The Albigensian Crusades [135]

The Cathars: The Struggle For, and of, A New Church [136]

---

[128] http://gordonnapierhistory.blogspot.com/2010/04/my-first-book-rise-and-fall-of-knights.html
[129] http://gnosistraditions.faithweb.com/mont.html
[130] http://bogomiltocathar.devhub.com/blog/category/albigensian-crusade/
[131] http://www.russianbooks.org/montsegur.htm
[132] http://www.crusades-encyclopedia.com/primarysourcesalbigensiancrusade.html
[133] http://www.bibliotecapleyades.net/esp_autor_whenry04.htm
[134] http://www.halexandria.org/dward220.htm
[135] http://xenophongroup.com/montjoie/albigens.htm
[136] http://www.philipcoppens.com/catharism.html

Vicarius Christi: The Vicar of Christ

The Church's War on The Cathars [137]

The Enigma of the Cathars, Part 1 [138]

The Enigma of the Cathars, Part 2 [139]

The Enigma of the Cathars, Part 3 [140]

The Enigma of the Cathars, Part 4 [141]

The Enigma of the Cathars, Part 5 [142]

The Enigma of the Cathars, Epilogue [143]

The Voice of the Cathars, Part 1 (by Louis Khourey) [144]

---

[137] http://newdawnmagazine.com.au/Article/The_Church_s_War_on_the_Cathars.html
[138] http://templeofpegasus.blogspot.com/2008/08/enigma-of-cathars-part-one.html
[139] http://templeofpegasus.blogspot.com/2008/08/enigma-of-cathars-part-two.html
[140] http://templeofpegasus.blogspot.com/2008/08/enigma-of-cathars-part-three.html
[141] http://templeofpegasus.blogspot.com/2008/09/enigma-of-cathars-part-four.html
[142] http://templeofpegasus.blogspot.com/2008/09/enigma-of-cathars-part-five.html
[143] http://templeofpegasus.blogspot.com/2008/09/enigma-of-cathars-epilogue.html
[144] http://tatfoundation.org/forum2001-06.htm

Vicarius Christi: The Vicar of Christ

The Voice of the Cathars, Part 2 (by Louis Khourey) [145]

The Voice of the Cathars, Part 3 (by Louis Khourey) [146]

Were the Templars Heretics? [147]

---

[145] http://tatfoundation.org/forum2001-07.htm
[146] http://tatfoundation.org/forum2001-08.htm
[147] http://blog.templarhistory.com/2010/03/were-the-templars-heretics/

Historical Fact

[1] The Roman Church was dedicated to wiping out the Messianic heirs (the descendants of Yeshua and his family).

[2] The Roman Church deliberately usurped the power of the Merovingian kings.

[3] The Roman Church directed specific brutal assaults against the Cathars, a peaceable Christian people.

[4] Women were "thoroughly disenfranchised and apart from Miriam-Mary, the mother of Jesus, were classed as harlots and whores;" [148] hence, the Witch hunts and the Witch burnings were primarily against females.

[5] The Roman Church deliberately tortured the Templar Knights.

Godfroi de Bouillon, said to be the founder of the Knights Templar, was of the Merovingian line.

---

[148] Vayro, Ian Ross. (2007) *God Save Us From Religion* (page 19). Queensland, Australia: Joshua Books.

Vicarius Christi: The Vicar of Christ

Born around 1060, he was "the second son of Eustace II, Count of Boulogne, and Ida of Lorraine (daughter of Godfrey III, Duke of Lower Lorraine and his wife, Doda)." [149] [150]

His father, Eustace II, Count of Boulogne, one of the few proven companions of William the Conqueror, is believed to have been the patron of the Bayeux Tapestry.

With fewer opportunities than his older brother, it appeared that he was "destined to become just one more minor knight in service to a rich landed nobleman. However, his uncle on his mother's side, Godfrey the Hunchback, Duke of Lower Lorraine, died childless and named his nephew, Godfrey of Bouillon, as his heir and next in line to his duchy of Lower Lorraine. This duchy was an important one at the time, serving as a buffer between the kingdom of France and the German lands." [151]

---

[149] http://en.wikipedia.org/wiki/Godfrey_of_Bouillon
[150] http://en.wikipedia.org/wiki/Godfrey_of_Bouillon#cite_note-Butler_93-0
[151] http://en.wikipedia.org/wiki/Godfrey_of_Bouillon

Vicarius Christi: The Vicar of Christ

In 1099, Godfroi de Bouillon, along with many landowners, became the leaders in the First Crusade; hence, the Chevaliers du Rocher de Sion (Knights of Mount Sion) were born. It was in Jerusalem, also during 1099, that Godfroi was appointed as the first Grand Master of the Order. By 1108, while in Palestine, some Knights of Zion, led by Hugues de Champagne, decided to change the name of the Order to Chevaliers du Temple de Jerusalem (Knights of the Temple in Jerusalem). [152]

It has been said that there are existing documents that claim that "the Order of Sion and the Order of the Temple (officially, the Poor Knights of the Temple of Solomon, later known as the Knights Templar, and officially recognized as such in 1118) were, until 1188, one unified organization with the same leadership." [153]

While Godfroi de Bouillon was the first ruler of the kingdom of Jerusalem, he was "unwilling to be called king

---

152

http://outlawjournalism.com/forum/viewtopic.php?f=6&t=6518&sid=a7e627d0215ef5a37434d6ada76ab01d&start=525
[153] http://www2.fiu.edu/~mizrachs/poseur3.html

Vicarius Christi: The Vicar of Christ

in the Holy Land since he regarded Jesus as the one and only king. Instead he called himself 'protector of the Holy Sepulcher' (*Advocatus Sancti Sepulchri*)." [154]

Godfroi's lineage flows thusly ……

King Childeric I

King Clovis I and St. Clothilde

King Clotaire I and Arégund von Thuringia

King Chilperic I and Fredegund

King Clotaire II and Haldetrude

King Dagobert I and Nanthilde

King Clovis II and Bathilde

---

[154] http://www.tacitus.nu/historical-atlas/regents/jerusalem.htm

Vicarius Christi: The Vicar of Christ

King Theuderic III and Clotilde of Heristal

Bertrada of Prüm (Merovingian princess) and Martin, Count of Laon

Charibert, Count of Laon and Bertrada of Cologne

Bertrada of Laon and Pépin III (the Short)

Holy Roman Emperor Charlemagne and Hildegard

Holy Roman Emperor Louis the Pious and Judith

Holy Roman Emperor Charles the Bald and Ermentrude of Orléans

Judith (daughter of Charles the Bald) and Baldwin I, Count of Flanders

* Through her marriage to two Kings of Wessex, Judith was twice a Queen, and through her third marriage to Baldwin, she became the first Countess of Flanders. She was ancestress of the later Counts of Flanders, as well as both stepmother and later the sister-in-law of King Alfred the Great.

Vicarius Christi: The Vicar of Christ

Baldwin II, Count of Flanders and Ælfthryth of Wessex (daughter of King Alfred the Great of the Saxons)

Adalof, Count of Boulogne

Arnulf II, Count of Boulogne

Arnulf III, Count of Boulogne

Baldwin II, Count of Boulogne and Adelina of Holland

Eustache I, Count of Boulogne and Matilda of Leuven (daughter of Lambert I, Count of Leuven, and Gerberga of Lower Lorraine)

Eustache II, Count of Boulogne and Ida of Lorraine (daughter of Godfrey III, Duke of Lower Lorraine and his wife, Doda)

Godfroi de Bouillon

Vicarius Christi: The Vicar of Christ

In summation, from the time of Byzantine Emperor Constantine I, and all in an effort "to prop up its fraudulent position, the Catholic Church began removing the competition with the war on descendents of Jesus, on heresy, magic and learning. From this time until around 1500 AD, the Catholics specifically targeted not only Manicheans, Cathars and Bogomils, but also Knights Templar, Jews (particularly Desposyni), Muslims and Gypsies [probably because occult wisdom and arcane secrets, attributed to Thoth Hermes Trismegistus, had been encoded in the Tarot cards]." [155]

According to author Tony Bushby, in the 1896 version of the Oxford Bible, "we can read, in Genesis 26:5, that the word Tarot is simply a plural form of Torah ... [a term that] refers to *The Law* ... [along] with a connotation of *instruction*." [156] In his book, The Secret of the Bible, Chapters 10 and 16 outline the correlation between the Tarot and the Bible.

---

[155] Vayro, Ian Ross. (2007) *God Save Us From Religion* (pages 189 and 190). Queensland, Australia: Joshua Books.
[156] Ibid, pages 279 and 280).

Vicarius Christi: The Vicar of Christ

A History and Mythos of the Knights Templar [157]

Clovis I to Godfroi [158]

Godfroi de Bouillon's Templar Knights: Mount Sion and the Essenes [159]

Knights Templar: The Historical Record [160]

The Burning Times: Description of the Phenomena [161]

The Burning Times: The Time Line (Dark Ages to now) [162]

The Crusades [163]

Malleus Maleficarum [164] [165] [166] [167]

---

[157] http://www.templarhistory.com/
[158] http://www.halexandria.org/dward217.htm
[159] http://www.thetemplebooklet.co.uk/GodfreyDeBoullionSandyHamblett.htm
[160] http://www.mastermason.com/hiramdiscovered/knightstemplar2.html
[161] http://www.religioustolerance.org/wic_burn1.htm
[162] http://www.religioustolerance.org/wic_burn2.htm
[163] http://boisestate.edu/courses/crusades/
[164] http://en.wikipedia.org/wiki/Malleus_Maleficarum
[165] http://www.sacred-texts.com/pag/mm/
[166] http://www.summerlands.com/crossroads/remembrance/_remembrance/malleus_maleficarum.htm
[167] http://www.bibliotecapleyades.net/cienciareal/cienciareal12.htm

Vicarius Christi: The Vicar of Christ

Malleus Maleficarum (Latin for *Hammer of the Witches*) [168]

The Witch Hunts (1400 to 1800 AD) [169]

The Witch Hunts: The End of Magic and Miracles [170]

Witch Hunt [171]

Witch Hunts and the Christian Mentality [172]

---

[168] http://www.reanimality.com/founders/mjd/writings/magick/malleusMaleficarum.pdf
[169] http://departments.kings.edu/womens_history/witch/
[170] http://www.thenazareneway.com/dark_side_of_christian_history.htm
[171] http://www.sacred-texts.com/pag/burning.htm
[172] http://www.atheistfoundation.org.au/articles/witch-hunts-and-christian-mentality

What Does This Mean?

When one reflects back on ...

[1] the forged Donation of Constantine

[2] the elimination of the Merovingian kings

[3] the installment of the Carolingian regime

[4] the establishment of church kingship

[5] the slaughtering of the Cathars

[6] the demise of the Knights Templar (in order to usurp their power and steal their vast wealth)

[7] the hateful Medieval Inquisition (a tribunal established for the sole purpose of discovery and punishment of heresy)

[8] the Papal Inquisition

[9] the determined dedication to wiping out the Desposyni (meaning the immediate heirs and relatives of Jesus)

Vicarius Christi: The Vicar of Christ

In truth, the fledging Church was "so terrified of the Holy Bloodline of Jesus that they claimed authenticity and descent from Peter," [173] a man who was *never* Pope. Linus, "the priestly second son of King Caradoc, was the *first* Pope actually appointed by Paul in 58 AD." [174]

[10] the persecution of early Christians

[11] the Witch hunts and the Witch burnings (mainly women)

[12] the selling of indulgences to finance the building of St. Peter's Basilica in Rome

[13] the removal, from the Bible, of things that might empower the individual (such as astrology, karma and reincarnation), only to replace them with devious and deceptive items (such as hell fire, damnation, Purgatory and the Devil), all in order to "ensure a confused and denigrated

---

[173] Vayro, Ian Ross. (2007) *God Save Us From Religion* (page 179). Queensland, Australia: Joshua Books.
[174] Ibid.

Vicarius Christi: The Vicar of Christ

congregation eternally subservient to, and reliant on, the clergy." [175]

[14] the fact that, in 318 AD, a delegation of Desposyni (blood relatives of Jesus) journeyed to Rome to seek audience with Bishop Sylvester, in the Lateran Palace, only to be told that "the teachings of Christ had been superseded by a doctrine that was more amenable to the requirements of Imperial Rome." [176] [177]

[15] the Council of Nicea, in 325 AD, whereby Constantine "sanctioned the confiscation and destruction of all earlier works that that might challenge the proto-orthodox teachings that came out of the Roman Church," [178] including those "classic works by pagan authors that referred to the historical Jesus." [179]

---

[175] Vayro, Ian Ross. (2007) *God Save Us From Religion* (page 19). Queensland, Australia: Joshua Books.
[176] Ibid, page 20.
[177] Vayro, Ian Ross. (2006) *They Lied To Us in Sunday School* (page 140). Queensland, Australia: Joshua Books.
[178] Vayro, Ian Ross. (2007) *God Save Us From Religion* (page 20). Queensland, Australia: Joshua Books.
[179] Ibid.

Vicarius Christi: The Vicar of Christ

This meant that any scripture that contradicted those chosen, for the newly developed canon of the Roman Church, was seized and suppressed. However, among the books "saved from the fire in the Alexandrian Library was a work entitled *The Life of Apollonius of Tyana*, written by Flavius Philostratus." [180] [181]

In this light, the current Bible was a cleverly manufactured one; a book that completely eliminated the divine feminine in order to create a patriarchal Church.

[16] the fact that there remains "enough evidence to believe that New Testament teachings stem not from Jesus, but rather from Apollonius of Tyana." [182]

[17] the fact that the Roman Catholic Church held onto the Dead Sea Scrolls for many years "before releasing their content, and then in a very controlled environment." [183]

---

[180] Vayro, Ian Ross. (2007) *God Save Us From Religion* (page 23). Queensland, Australia: Joshua Books.
[181] Vayro, Ian Ross. (2006) *They Lied To Us in Sunday School* (page 146). Queensland, Australia: Joshua Books.
[182] Vayro, Ian Ross. (2007) *God Save Us From Religion* (page 24). Queensland, Australia: Joshua Books.

Vicarius Christi: The Vicar of Christ

[18] the disenfranchisement of women in being classified as *unclean* harlots and whores, all save the mother of Jesus (which actually encouraged homosexuality, sodomy and debauchery amongst Popes and clergy) [184]

… it is quite clear that the Roman Church, whether you choose to believe it or not, had a political agenda; an agenda that still continues into the present day.

Byzantine Emperor Constantine I saw that "he could gain political expediency within his Empire if he could unite the people with one doctrine. In 325 AD, at the Council of Nicea, he gathered together some 1,786 learned men, including at least 300 Bishops, from the various countries within the Empire in order to standardize religious worship. It was an extremely clever maneuver by the Emperor to have the State take over the religion of the masses." [185]

---

[183] Vayro, Ian Ross. (2007) *God Save Us From Religion* (page 24). Queensland, Australia: Joshua Books.
[184] Ibid, page 181.
[185] Vayro, Ian Ross. (2008) *Tears in Heaven* (page 25). Queensland, Australia: Joshua Books.

Vicarius Christi: The Vicar of Christ

Constantine both sanctioned and supplied "the finances to print copies of a Latin *Bible* [if you will] in 331 AD that featured the newly selected works, plus the fraudulent Roman prepared material. This enabled the custodians of the new 'orthodoxy' to revise, edit, and rewrite their material as they saw fit." [186]

Constantine was the authority who determined *what* was to be included and *how* it was to be written; hence, the Bible was composed and compiled by "intimidated and fallible men with vested interests and a particular job to do for the Roman Empire." [187]

The Roman Church, itself, was a *manufactured* doctrine, a doctrine of alterations and distortions, a doctrine created around money and power, based on the original Hebrew message now deemed heretical; a doctrine also adopting many Jewish patriarchs, including Adam, Seth, Noah,

---

[186] Vayro, Ian Ross. (2008) *Tears in Heaven* (page 30). Queensland, Australia: Joshua Books.
[187] Ibid.

Vicarius Christi: The Vicar of Christ

Abraham, Jacob, Joseph, Moses, King David, Solomon and John the Baptist.[188]

In addition, they also "adopted the Jewish Rabbi, Jesus Christ (who was rejected as the Messiah by the Jews), gave him a 'face-lift' and worked hard to remove any trace of Jewishness"[189] from his New Testament avatar unveiling.

Having arrived at their doctrine prototype, "they classified anyone with differing views as heretics, and quite effectively eliminated the competition. Hundreds of thousands of innocent have people died in the various purges and inquisitions because of differing beliefs. People are still dying today because of differing beliefs and the score is now in the tens of millions."[190]

What is truly misleading and horrendous about all of this is the very fact that individuals are brainwashed to believe that

---

[188] Vayro, Ian Ross. (2008) *Tears in Heaven* (page 30). Queensland, Australia: Joshua Books.
[189] Ibid.
[190] Ibid, page 31.

in killing others they are serving God in their noble cause and divinely inspired mission.

Quite the marketing scheme, one that keeps the greater multitude subservient to the few, wouldn't you say?

It was the Danish philosopher, theologian and religious author, Søren Kierkegaard (1813 to 1855) who suggested that religion "has now become escapism and entertainment for a congregation seeking magic without, rather than seeking things of God within." [191]

Organized religion clearly manipulates the masses through the controlling of minds, akin to a herd mentality, which most effectively limits one's thinking.

Perhaps it has now come down to the saying that *people who live in glass houses should not throw stones*, a most apt descriptor of these times.

---

[191] Vayro, Ian Ross. (2008) *Tears in Heaven* (page 129). Queensland, Australia: Joshua Books.

Vicarius Christi: The Vicar of Christ

Spurious Origins of the English Church and its Royal Lineages, Part 1 [192]

Spurious Origins of the English Church and its Royal Lineages, Part 2 [193]

Spurious Origins of the English Church and its Royal Lineages, Part 3 [194]

Spurious Origins of the English Church and its Royal Lineages, Explanatory Notes [195]

The Bible Fraud Related Reports [196]

The Digital Dead Sea Scrolls [197]

---

[192] http://www.tonybushby.com/articles/view/8
[193] http://www.tonybushby.com/articles/view/9
[194] http://www.tonybushby.com/articles/view/10
[195] http://www.tonybushby.com/articles/view/11
[196] http://www.bibliotecapleyades.net/esp_biblianazar.htm#The_Bible_Fraud_Related_Reports
[197] http://dss.collections.imj.org.il/isaiah

Vicarius Christi: The Vicar of Christ

The Hidden Agenda of The Passion of the Christ [198]

The Kentroversy Papers [199]

The Life of Apollonius of Tyana [200]

The Piso Family and The Story of the Bible [201]

The Roman Piso Homepage [202]

Tony Bushby Blog [203]

Who Created The Catholic Church? [204]

---

[198] http://www.retakingamerica.com/article_passion_hidden_agenda.html
[199] http://kentroversypapers.blogspot.com/2007/04/book-review-twin-deception-by-tony.html
[200] http://www.livius.org/ap-ark/apollonius/apollonius_life.html
[201] http://www.bibliotecapleyades.net/esp_sociopol_piso.htm
[202] http://www.angelfire.com/biz5/piso/
[203] http://www.tonybushby.com/blog
[204] http://www.bibliotecapleyades.net/vatican/esp_vatican43.htm

Doom and Gloom Hype

The different religions and philosophies around the world "are plainly in conflict with each other, and quite apparently, this divergence is not without a reason" [205] meaning that everyone is convinced that *their* belief system is the correct one, and that all of the others are wrong, thereby preventing "any investigation of their own doctrine or the consideration of anything outside." [206] A rather ingenious plan, really.

One is not encouraged to explore the deeper connections associated with spirituality; instead, one is committed to paying the mortgage, feeding the family, clothing the family, educating the children, encouraging the children to become involved in extra-curricular activities ... all of which leaves very little time to delve into matters of a spiritual nature. [207]

In order to escape the doom and gloom programming that exists, one must learn to reconfigure their mind.

---

[205] Vayro, Ian Ross. (2008) *Tears in Heaven* (page 412). Queensland, Australia: Joshua Books.
[206] Ibid.
[207] Ibid.

Vicarius Christi: The Vicar of Christ

This becomes the period that I refer to as the crossing of the threshold; a time whereby you are faced with a major decision – to either continue as is, in your stress filled life, or forge ahead, into the realm of the unexplored, all in an effort to rediscover *who* you really are.

It is so very true that guilty and fearful people are very easy to control; at least, this has been my personal experience regarding the Roman Catholic religion.

Fear and guilt were additional perks added to the manufactured doctrinal package, further highlighting that "restitution and salvation could only take place underneath the umbrella of the church." [208]

This meant that God could either "reward you or punish you by sending you to heaven or hell depending on how you adhered to the dogmas and doctrines of the church." [209]

---

[208] Bunick, Nick. (1998) *In God's Truth* (page 161). Charlottesville, VA: Hampton Roads Publishing Corporation, Inc.
[209] Ibid.

Vicarius Christi: The Vicar of Christ

In addition, it was proclaimed "that all are in sin the moment they exit from their mothers' wombs ... condemned to go to hell for this sin ... unless they became a member of the church and were baptized." [210]

Taking his invention further, Augustine shared that "Adam committed the first sin when he ate the apple in the Garden of Eden, and we are all a product of Adam's sperm." [211] This was his way of stating that "Adam's sin corrupted the body and soul of the whole human race," [212] further culminating in the need to be baptized free of the sin of disobedience; hence, the birth of guilt through original sin.

I grew up believing in a punishing God (the heaven versus hell premise). I was also brought up to believe in the idea that an evil force, supernatural in nature, was competing against God for my soul. Between the Devil and Purgatory, I didn't know which was worse.

---

[210] Bunick, Nick. (1998) *In God's Truth* (page 161). Charlottesville, VA: Hampton Roads Publishing Corporation, Inc.
[211] Ibid, pages 161 and 162.
[212] Ibid, page 162.

Likewise, I was brought up to believe that Jesus died for my sins because I was born into sin.

What one has to learn, first and foremost, is how to release one's self from these herd (*baa-baa*) mentality controls.

How, then, do we go about releasing ourselves from this collective bondage of fear?

How do we go about creating and maintaining a positive, more optimistic, mindset?

Consciousness is an extension of mind.

The act of focusing your consciousness, then, is also an act of creation, meaning that consciousness creates.

Everything you are witness to in your own life was, first and foremost, a thought. This is why it becomes so absolutely crucial to *become aware of what you think*.

Everything about you can change from one moment to the next (thoughts, feelings and emotions), depending on what your consciousness is focused upon.

Vicarius Christi: The Vicar of Christ

Your emotions determine the effectiveness of your actions.

Negative states only serve to make you feel increasingly stuck, whereas positive states are empowering. Spending time with supportive and positive people helps keep one positive.

Affirmations have been proven to work for those who feel and believe in the words (messages) they are reciting to themselves. While affirmations can be utilized throughout the day, they are <u>even more effective</u> if stated *before you go to sleep* given the fact that brain activity slows down when you are entering the Alpha brainwave level (the necessary level for reprogramming and rewiring your brain), a state of physical and mental relaxation.

In conjunction with creative visualization, the power of thought can be used to manifest dreams and create change.

It is important to remember that no one thinks the exact same thoughts the way you do; hence, there is no one that sends out the exact same vibrational frequencies that you do.

Vicarius Christi: The Vicar of Christ

I was incredibly excited to see this described as a *mental fingerprint*, [213] meaning that everything connected to you is unique.

Thoughts and ideas are energy. They are the building blocks of creation. One must first have the thought before it can be manifested into form. To have the thought, one must first have mind.

All of creation (meaning form) is the product of mind and thought; hence, all of creation is the product of imagination. Mind, therefore, can be said to be the very catalyst behind everything in existence.

Every thought you have, has the power to influence events in either a positive or negative way. Your thoughts and beliefs create situations. What you experience is up to you.

You already have all the power you need to create all of the changes that you wish for yourself. It is the focus of your awareness (mindfulness) that will become the reality of your world.

---

[213] http://www.one-mind-one-energy.com/unique.html

Vicarius Christi: The Vicar of Christ

Change can only begin from within. This has been the route of my personal journey.

Understanding "the power of beliefs and the power of the mind, both individually and en masse, is the most pressing and crucial issue for humankind to grasp." [214]

Marciniak succinctly shares that "developing the ability to become aware of what you think, feel, and speak, and structuring your life with pristine clarity through thought, word, and deed are of essential importance for living an empowered life." [215] Likewise, "accepting responsibility for the power you embody is the essential and most important lesson of this transformation." [216]

Marciniak writes that "questioning everything – your life, your beliefs, and your world view – is the most essential part of the process of discovering your inherent power to create the world you meet. It takes great courage to question your

---

[214] Marciniak, Barbara. (2004). *Path of Empowerment: New Pleiadian Wisdom for a World in Chaos* (page 5). Novato, CA: New World Library.
[215] Ibid, page 6.
[216] Ibid.

existence, and even greater strength is required to know and recognize the truth when you see it." [217]

This power becomes even more pronounced "when millions of people focus their attention upon listening to the same words, seeing the same pictures, and hearing the same descriptions ... [because] tremendous energy is generated and a massive thought-form is created. Thought-forms are vibrational blueprints that hold instructions for manifesting reality. The media captures your attention and then programs your imagination, essentially canceling out your unique creative drive to manifest your own reality as well as your desire to know yourself. You have been conditioned to believe that all you need to know can now be found in the wonderful world of electronic boxes and the information and entertainment they contain. When "the news" is slanted toward a message of continuous war, a state of despair and a sense of hopelessness are created. A paralysis of power takes hold because you become convinced that the only

---

[217] Marciniak, Barbara. (2004). *Path of Empowerment: New Pleiadian Wisdom for a World in Chaos* (page 15). Novato, CA: New World Library.

Vicarius Christi: The Vicar of Christ

reality is what is described and prescribed by the authorities in the box ... [when, in retrospect], reality is created and produced by each and every one of you, and those seeking to control the world have kept this knowledge a well-guarded secret." [218]

We have been told what to think, what to believe, how to act, what to say, and how to respond – all courtesy of our leaders. Not an accusation, this has been our current reality for thousands of years. We have settled for the status quo, *until now.*

Take the time to imagine the flip-side of what we have been told to think and believe. In wanting to venture forth, there are some very important questions that must be asked.

[1] Am I sure that I really want to go there?

[2] Do I want to rattle the bars of my self-imposed cage?

---

[218] Marciniak, Barbara. (2004). *Path of Empowerment: New Pleiadian Wisdom for a World in Chaos* (page 31). Novato, CA: New World Library.

Vicarius Christi: The Vicar of Christ

[3] Do I wish to expand my mind by thinking outside the box?

[4] Do I wish to enhance my conscious awareness to include new vistas of information?

[5] Do I wish to refine my individual frequency band, my personal energy signature?

[6] Do I wish to fine tune my perceptions?

[7] Do I wish to identify hidden meanings of life?

[8] Do I wish to fully participate in life?

[9] Do I wish to observe my interactions without judgment?

[10] Do I wish to be awakened?

[11] Do I wish to experience complete and total freedom?

Having long been controlled through fear and guilt, your heart will tell you when it is time to forge ahead. As to bravery, only time will tell, as each strives to break free from an ancient spell that has been in place for thousands of years.

Vicarius Christi: The Vicar of Christ

Marciniak says that "you must first learn to manage your attention in the here and now in order to become much more aware of the language of frequencies. Inner signals and messages are effortlessly and generously transmitted by everyone." [219]

Many are aware that love is the vital-force energy that sustains all life. We were created in love. We come from love. We are love.

In learning to both cultivate and feel a genuine love and appreciation for who we are in this physical embodiment, we are able to more fully connect with this energy, contributing our own version of this love frequency to this 3D reality.

So where does one actually start?

[1] First and foremost, one starts by realizing that personal change is imminent.

---

[219] Marciniak, Barbara. (2004). *Path of Empowerment: New Pleiadian Wisdom for a World in Chaos* (page 21). Novato, CA: New World Library.

[2] It then advances to positive thinking, something that can be difficult, but not impossible, to achieve.

How can this be so, you ask?

A positive outlook "is a symptom of maturity, which takes time and conscious effort to develop. You have to uproot old attitudes and resolve deep-seated misunderstandings about life. As long as you feel angry, you can think wishful thoughts all you want, but nothing will happen. Positive thinking means learning to face the material in your shadows. You need to be whole, inside, if you want your affirmations to work." [220]

Muster continues by saying that "whenever you hold something in the spotlight of your awareness, you are using the power of the conscious mind. Thousands of thoughts go through your mind every day, like a raging river of thought. However, if you do not pay attention to what you think, you may waste this valuable resource dwelling on useless

---

[220] Muster, Nori. (2007). Dreaming Peace: Introduction. Retrieved February 2, 2008, from http://surrealist.org/writing/dreamingpeaceintro.html

negative things like worry and gossip. If you want to use the power of your mind for your benefit, you need to change your thoughts. To improve your thoughts, you first have to be aware of what they are. If you learn to change your mind through positive autosuggestion, you can change your reality too." [221]

While becoming aware of your thoughts is a time consuming process, it is absolutely essential. Do not expect this to be an easy process. You must focus on taking baby steps, one day at a time, in an effort to counteract your thinking.

In essence, it is much akin to reconfiguring your brain whilst, at the same time, dismantling, but not destroying, the ego, which is a painful process, even when one deems themselves ready and up to the challenge.

Where does the subconscious mind come into play in keeping with one's thoughts, you ask?

---

[221] Muster, Nori. (2007). How Positive Thinking Works, Part 1: Autosuggestion. Retrieved February 2, 2008, from http://surrealist.org/writing/dreamingpeace1.html

Vicarius Christi: The Vicar of Christ

The subconscious tries to help by showing us the truth, attempting to communicate through our dreams and gut feelings that, while painful, can be viewed as a trustworthy friend.

The subconscious knows "everything about you and records every thought, picture, and feeling you think. You need to be aware of your feelings and be responsible for them." [222]

In continuation, Muster shares that "it may be difficult to recognize the negative mental attitudes you have acquired. They may seem so familiar that you take them for granted. You may wake up with a vague feeling of foreboding. You may be overcome with worry or raw feelings about money. You may feel so angry about some aspect of your life that you can't imagine living without the anger. However, once you have some experience using autosuggestion, you will realize these are just thoughts in the mind ... deeply embedded patterns attached to neurons with negative programming. You can change them because you are the

---

[222] Muster, Nori. (2007). How Positive Thinking Works, Part 1: Autosuggestion. Retrieved February 2, 2008, from http://surrealist.org/writing/dreamingpeace1.html

one who decides what thoughts to keep. You have the ability to change anything about your inner life if you make a conscious effort."[223]

Let's face it; mental attitudes are often difficult to change because they are generally based on one's underlying beliefs. To change and/or challenge one's mental attitude(s) in order to develop positive thinking, one must question their belief system(s), and most would rather not do so. It can be a painful, albeit necessary, process.

Muster discusses negative mental states (all of which embody such things as fear, unproductive worrying, excessive worrying, perfectionism, jealousy, anger, resentment, chronic victim hood, loneliness, emptiness and superstitions) in greater depth, all of which can control one to such a degree that they become completely paralyzed.

Love is an exceptionally big part of positive thinking.

---

[223] Muster, Nori. (2007). How Positive Thinking Works, Part 11: Positive Mental Attitude. Retrieved February 2, 2008, from http://surrealist.org/writing/dreamingpeace2.html

Vicarius Christi: The Vicar of Christ

You have to both love and accept yourself, all facets of yourself, the light as well as the dark, in order to begin experiencing what has been referred to as your higher purpose.

While interpersonal relationships also figure into positive thinking, one also has to learn to be themselves, to learn to remain true to who they are by listening to their heart, in order to most effectively deal with a situation that may arise.

If one tries to blend in and/or conform to the expectations of another, they end up consigning themselves to the world of 'mediocrity' as shared by Muster.

In having entered the love (positive thinking) paradigm, which may be a complete shift for some people, you continue to set an example for others.

"Although things may look bleak ... with endless wars, the threat of terrorism, diminishing natural resources, catastrophic weather events ... good things can happen too.

Vicarius Christi: The Vicar of Christ

There are tremendous challenges; but when enough people hold a vision of love, it will happen." [224]

If indeed "we want to create a peaceful world, then we must set an example of what it is like to live by peaceful ideals. In the peace paradigm, humanity is one people and everyone is part of the whole." [225]

Raised within the Catholic faith, like Steve Pavlina, I was able to reprogram my religious beliefs, a process that spanned years.

I began my Gnostic search, seeking my own inner truth, based on what resonated within the core of my being.

Delving into the so-called New Age realm, I ended up taking a bit from many disciplines in order to create my new belief system. Almost immediately, I began attracting like-minded individuals into my life.

---

[224] Muster, Nori. (2007). How Positive Thinking Works, Part IV: Solve Collective Problems. Retrieved February 2, 2008, from http://surrealist.org/writing/dreamingpeace4.html
[225] Ibid.

It was likewise for Pavlina who shares that he came to understand that "instead of your beliefs being based on reality, they're creating your reality." [226]

Things begin to get more interesting when Pavlina says that "I can't prove to you that you're in a thought bubble right now, but you can prove it to yourself if you have enough curiosity to make the attempt. You have to decide to swallow the red pill. The only way to prove you're in a thought bubble is to consciously change your thoughts in such a way that you contradict at least one of the foundational beliefs that form the bubble. This begins with opening your mind to the possibility that your thoughts are shaping your reality." [227]

In stepping outside preconceived beliefs, as governed by the Matrix, one is able to contradict many foundational beliefs that exist within this controlled environment.

---

[226] Pavlina, Steve. (2005). Take the Red Pill. Retrieved February 2, 2008, from http://www.stevepavlina.com/blog/2005/03/take-the-red-pill/
[227] Ibid.

Vicarius Christi: The Vicar of Christ

While I do not know to what degree our thoughts create our reality, like Pavlina, I am also convinced "beyond a reasonable doubt, that our thoughts have a strong and powerful effect on creating the reality we experience. I don't know how deep the rabbit hole goes. I'm sitting in a thought bubble of my own, and, as such, my own reality is being shaped by the nature of that bubble." [228]

As long as one completely adheres to rigid dogma and a closed mind, one can never take back their power.

The time has come for each of you to believe that you are in control, that you have "all the answers. You are the centre of your own universe and you can make it whatever you choose. You are simply incredible. Feel it, live it and your world will be transformed." [229]

Now is the time to reclaim the power that you have given away.

---

[228] Pavlina, Steve. (2005). Take the Red Pill. Retrieved February 2, 2008, from http://www.stevepavlina.com/blog/2005/03/take-the-red-pill/
[229] Icke, David. (1999). *The Biggest Secret* (page 488). Scottsdale, AZ: Bridge of Love Publications USA.

Vicarius Christi: The Vicar of Christ

How does one go about reclaiming their power, so as to begin thinking anew for themselves?

David Icke makes note of several noteworthy steps.

"Step One: Refuse to have another tell you what to think and do with your life. What matters [most] is that you are you, and not what someone else is telling you to be. Respect the freedom of others to do the same." [230]

Remain true to yourself by listening to your heart.

"Step Two: As the process of unplugging continues, things that mattered to you before become less important and your outlook on life, and others, starts to transform. You become more tolerant of yourself and others. Your attitudes to[wards] everything change once the recognition of the illusion goes deeper and deeper and you start to be that awareness, rather than just intellectually accepting its existence. Don't think it, know it; don't try to do it, just do it. These are very different states of being. When you

---

[230] Icke, David. (1999). *The Biggest Secret* (page 444). Scottsdale, AZ: Bridge of Love Publications USA.

become more consciously aware of the illusion, you can begin to enjoy it without all the hang-ups that imprison us when we think it is real. We can have fun and express our desires, as long as they don't impinge on the freedom of others." [231]

This means that *we are here to live and partake of the now.* We must cease the unproductive and unnecessary worry. We are here to learn to trust in the greater power of the Universe.

"Step Three: Taking ... responsibility and ceasing to blame others – or ourselves – is to take a massive step on the freedom road. The most destructive expression of this is blaming others for our plight. In truth, only we have that power if we choose to use it; but if we believe that others are in control of our destiny, we will create that reality.

---

[231] Icke, David. (2003). *Tales from The Time Loop* (pages 445 to 448). Wildwood, MO: Bridge of Love Publications USA.

"Step Four: We need to start focusing on the right to freedom of expression" [232] for all.

As long as we believe that division and separateness exists, the Matrix has us and owns us, for it alone promotes this duality.

Oneness = Love = Balance

Hatred = Illusion of Division = Disharmony

Marciniak is also in complete agreement, sharing that "you can change any situation by changing your previous attitudes and expectations. Refocusing your attention and consciously selecting your thoughts to reinforce the outcome you desire will alter the frequency you transmit, inevitably opening the door to another probable outcome. Reality

---

[232] Icke, David. (2003). *Tales from The Time Loop* (pages 445 to 448). Wildwood, MO: Bridge of Love Publications USA.

adjusting, or using your frequency by way of intent, is the wave of the future." [233]

When we focus on something, we give power to the vibrations. In essence, these ideas ultimately become our truth. This is an accurate definition for both positive and negative thoughts.

You simply end up creating more of the same, depending on the nature of your focus.

What we believe, we bring into being. By focusing on abundance rather than lack, we can enjoy a reality in alignment with positive energies and new beginnings.

If we want to see more love in the world, we must become love. If we want to see more peace in this world, we must become peace. If we want to see more compassion in this world, we must become compassion.

Simply put, *we must become that which we seek.*

---

[233] Marciniak, Barbara. (2004). *Path of Empowerment: New Pleiadian Wisdom for a World in Chaos* (page 50). Novato, CA: New World Library.

Vicarius Christi: The Vicar of Christ

Unplugging from the Matrix, from the illusion that we have long considered real, is not an easy road for most.

What does it involve?

No problem can be solved from the same level of consciousness that created it. These powerful words were uttered by Albert Einstein.

There are a number of "versions of what Einstein is supposed to have said, but this one encapsulates all of them. In short, the problems that we see in this world, this *reality*, cannot be repaired by the same kind of thinking [sense of reality] that created them. Why? Because the 'world' is a reflection of that 'thinking' and if the 'thinking' doesn't change, neither can its reflection, meaning the 'world'. The manipulators understand this and they are constantly offering and encouraging 'solutions' that they know will just exacerbate the problems and create more." [234]

---

[234] David Icke Newsletter. Received via email on February 3, 2008, from http://www.davidicke.com/

Vicarius Christi: The Vicar of Christ

Round and round we go "and so it must be because the global merry-go-round is just a manifestation of thought processes, individual and collective, going round and round, repeating, repeating, repeating. As the saying goes – *If you always do what you've always done, you'll always get what you've always got.* Put another way – If you think what you've always thought, you'll create what you've always created." [235]

Unless one wants to be stuck in the same mindset, day after day, year after year, lifetime after lifetime, a consciousness shift, outside of the ever repeating cycle [meaning that we are trying to solve problems with the same level of consciousness that created them], is needed in order to trigger any transformation of the current reality.

True Love, however, "has a different agenda. True Love creates reality and True Love creates opportunities. Trust in

---

[235] David Icke Newsletter. Received via email on February 3, 2008, from http://www.davidicke.com/

the voice of your beloved one inside your heart. This voice never lies. Trust in yourself." [236]

In keeping, True Love is stronger than the Matrix system of control.

Love, in its truest and most infinite sense, "is not a spectator, not some inactive esoteric concept. It is the ultimate power in all existence and it is there for everyone to connect with, and express, in daily experience whenever we choose. The tragic thing is that we don't choose and that's why we have the world that we do." [237]

Become Conscious.

These two words will assist in the transformation of our current reality to something much more, to something that is equated with love and respect.

---

[236] The Rules of the Matrix. Retrieved on February 2, 2008, from http://www.geocities.com/freeyourbrain/rules.htm

[237] David Icke Newsletter. Received via email on February 3, 2008, from http://www.davidicke.com/

Vicarius Christi: The Vicar of Christ

These particular values "are the soul mates of awakened consciousness and they will transform this ball of division and conflict into the paradise it is destined to be. Paradise is not a place; it is a state of being that transcends all places, races and expressions of the Infinite." [238]

In practical terms, this means "doing what you *know* to be right rather than what you *think* is right for you in the moment," [239] with right meaning in reference to your heart.

What does your heart tell you is the right course of action? Let's not kid ourselves into thinking "that we don't know what the heart is saying. We do – it's just that its urgings are ignored because the head is saying: What are the consequences here for me?" [240]

It is the system, known as the Matrix, that urges us to put the self first; hence, division and separateness continue to rule supreme.

---

[238] David Icke Newsletter. Received via email on February 3, 2008, from http://www.davidicke.com/
[239] Ibid.
[240] Ibid.

Vicarius Christi: The Vicar of Christ

By comparison, love urges us to see that "we are all One and that therefore the greater good and the 'individual' good are indivisible." [241]

Just imagine "the transformation of daily life that would emerge from the values of love and doing what we *know to be right* and not what we think is right for us. Unfairness and injustice would fade away, and so would conflict, war and imposition of will." [242]

There will be times when "it will be right to defend yourself against injustice and stand your ground in the name of fairness. Other times, it will be right to concede your own position and desires [in order] to provide fairness and justice for another." [243]

We are able to create such a world when we begin by engaging in a completely different state of being; by doing what we *know* to be right and fair.

---

[241] David Icke Newsletter. Received via email on February 3, 2008, from http://www.davidicke.com/
[242] Ibid.
[243] Ibid.

Vicarius Christi: The Vicar of Christ

In essence, *we become conscious*, and, in so doing, are able to demonstrate opening the channels to higher consciousness. The energy that is carried by our intent "cracks the auric eggshells of body consciousness and sets us free of the system's 'values' that are designed to enslave us in me, me, me." [244]

Are you now beginning to envision what the gifts of love and respect can give to the world, "a world in which everyone does what they like as long as they don't impose it on anyone else? Diversity of view and lifestyle can live in harmony so long as love and respect hold the balance between them. It brings together both respect for our right to do and be what we choose, while respecting those same rights for others, and it will bring an end to the complexity that engulfs us today," [245] keeping us prisoner.

The system loves complexity because it entraps the mind. We remain bewildered in that the problems are too big and there is nothing that we can do, leading to inaction.

---

[244] David Icke Newsletter. Received via email on February 3, 2008, from http://www.davidicke.com/
[245] Ibid.

Vicarius Christi: The Vicar of Christ

Can any of this be accomplished with the level of today's collective consciousness?

Once again, we are back to Albert Einstein for our answer: *No problem can be solved from the same level of consciousness that created it.*

This also means that reality cannot be transformed "by the same level of consciousness that enslaved it." [246]

The consciousness shift that is needed is coming. We are awakening to a new point of observation.

The biggest challenge for all of us, in this time of much needed transition, is *to live our words and not just speak them.*

Humans have developed a wondrous gift for self-deception and we are simply brilliant at persuading ourselves that what we think is right for us is what is right for the greater good.

The time, to be honest with ourselves, is now.

---

[246] David Icke Newsletter. Received via email on February 3, 2008, from http://www.davidicke.com/

Vicarius Christi: The Vicar of Christ

Eckhart Tolle, author of <u>A New Earth: Awakening To Your Life's Purpose</u>, was the forefront guest on Oprah, courtesy of a live world wide web event. [247]

No matter where in the world you were living at that time, you were able to participate, courtesy of your computer.

I completely acknowledge and concur with The Big Lie (both *attachment to the ego* as well as *separation from the Infinite Source*) that we have been fed in this current dreamstate for thousands and thousands of years, the basis of *Our Current Collective Reality Is Most Shocking Indeed*, an essay of mine. In keeping, I made a conscious decision to reclaim my power.

I am currently able to observe my own thoughts within a much increased state of detached neutrality, only because I was able to reconfigure my thoughts, my words, my reactions; a process that took years.

---

[247] http://www.oprah.com/oprahsbookclub/Your-Personal-Workbook-for-A-New-Earth

Vicarius Christi: The Vicar of Christ

No longer asleep, I can completely attest to the fact that when one begins to get out of their own way (the dissolving of the ego), they begin to develop a trust beyond who they thought they once were.

As Eckhart Tolle states, *it is this refinement that will serve to change the collective consciousness of the planet.*

All of the individual fears, doubts, angers, jealousies and resentments contribute to the collective consciousness. In keeping, therefore, each individual must step out of their own egoic consciousness, in order to begin to change themselves.

In so doing, they also begin to change the collective. Even the tiniest ripple can elicit a wave of change.

My focus has since become needing to reach that place, within, that is unconditioned and formless (spirit), inviting stillness into my life.

I am no longer as interested in worldly things. Not sure where this will take me, I am willing to step out of my own way in order to continue to learn see with enhanced clarity.

Vicarius Christi: The Vicar of Christ

For the true power within to shine forth, the ego has to die. One is then resurrected, and reconnected, with their very soul.

Could this be what has long been meant by the cryptic, and very much paraphrased, words attributed to Jesus – the importance of living in the world and yet not being a part of the world?

In each of the sixteen chapters of <u>The Secret in The Bible</u>, "one special word is written with something different about its presentation ... NoT misprints or typing errors ... but intentionally altered or 'coded' to spell out a special message." [248] In keeping, "those persons who search and record them in the order presented will find revealed a deep ancient secret that was extracted from the ancient *Book of God*, a mysterious old document written on a fabric of an unknown nature, and highly regarded by the Ancients, thousands of years ago." [249]

---

[248] Bushby, Tony. (2003). *The Secret in The Bible* (page 6). Queensland, Australia: Joshua Books.
[249] Ibid.

It is further shared that these "coded clues are called *Words of Truth* and there is no glamorous earthly prize for their discovery, excepting hidden treasure to nourish the Soul." [250]

Herein lies the special message contained within the text.

Learn deeply of the mind and its mystery for therein lies the true secret of immortality.

This clearly means that we need not look outside of ourselves for the answers that we seek. All that we need resides within. One merely needs to embrace the silence, the stillness, the unconditioned, the formless, the spirit, the void, in order to go to the place where the mind is no longer operating. A place where all is still without thinking, where one will be able to reconnect with the very essence and sacredness of their being; a place that can only be reached by being still.

Eckhart Tolle shares that this is a place where you are more alert than when you are thinking.

---

[250] Bushby, Tony. (2003). *The Secret in The Bible* (page 6). Queensland, Australia: Joshua Books.

Vicarius Christi: The Vicar of Christ

Spirituality has *nothing* to do with what you believe and *everything* to do with your state of consciousness.

The basis for all life is the present moment; acceptance of the moment as it is. Gratitude is also a significant part of this enhanced awareness.

In speaking for myself, I am finally ready to be still. I am finally ready to be present in the moment; to be at peace with what is.

It doesn't matter if an individual "cannot alter the world or individually change the System. What matters is that whatever the individual does, they do it from the heart, with loving intent. Only then will changes become noticeable. Only then will the individual begin to tap into their true source of power – that which lies within. If we do not tap into this inner core, we will never synchronize with our true potential, and that unique inspiration will never come to the fore to be realized and worked with. Until that happens we will always be manipulated by whoever has the will to control us. We will always be 'followers' and clones, reactionary beings, and not what we are supposed to be:

unique creators and channels for the Source into this world of matter." [251]

Fraser goes further to say that "the only advice I am going to give is advice which I believe will empower people to find their own power. From that position comes enlightenment. With enlightenment comes escape from the reliance on others because at the end of the day, all evolution and creation comes from within." [252]

His advice follows herein.

1. Look upon every man, woman and child as your equal. We are all from the same Source, and your love for them will help them to harmonize with yours and their inner spirit which is One in the Source.

2. Respect their right to individuality. You don't have to agree with them. You don't even have to like what they do or believe. However you respond to what they do or

---

[251] Fraser, Ivan. "Love Changes Everything". The Truth Campaign magazine. September 2000: Volume 17, page 49.
[252] Ibid.

what they stand for, never lose sight of the fact that you and they are spiritual kin. We have a right not to agree and to dislike another's actions and beliefs, but to hate another is like hating a part of one's own body.

3. Love yourself. This will plug your awareness into your heart center. It will enable clarity of thought and perception. The ultimate realization here is the fact that by truly loving another, you are loving yourself.

4. Make everything you do a dedication to the affirmation: May this be for *the greater good of all*. **When you affirm this, make sure it is drawn from within in accordance with The Source of All Truth and Light.** [253]

5. Remember, you have absolute freewill. That freewill includes the opportunity to choose to live in service for the greater good of all. You don't have to become a martyr. Just become who and what you already are and align with the Source in your daily life.

---

[253] Fraser, Ivan. "Love Changes Everything". <u>The Truth Campaign</u> magazine. September 2000: Volume 17, pages 49 and 50.

6. Choose to live according to the heart first, rather than the head first. The two need to be balanced, and spirit must be grounded, but the heart knows far more than the head, and, if trusted, can lead to remarkably wonderful synchronicities and realizations. The inner spirit is your connection with the Source, the Godhead.

7. Of course, there must be a degree of sacrifice. We cannot gain without giving and we cannot take just because we want, for it is the over-stimulation of 'want' which has led us to become so out of balance with our true selves. Over-stimulated want comes from the desire to control and this comes from the need of the ego; the ego must always be kept in check and guided by our inner awareness. When the heart says 'give' then it is time to give, so give generously of your time and energy to others who need it. But do not do it to the detriment of yourself – which you will not if you love and respect yourself as much as you love and respect others.

8. Appreciate, everyday, what you have.

9. Remember to find time to be still and quiet to allow the inner voice to speak to you.

10. Speak your truth openly and do not fear what others may think of you in consequence. Avoid lying to others, as lies create imbalance and carry karmic energy which eventually rebounds upon the liar.

11. Face every adversity as a learning experience. Only you can decide whether an experience is there to face or avoid. Only love of the self and others will bring forth the realization of how to deal with any situation correctly.

12. Never allow guilt to interfere with your life. If you have erred, learn from it and give thanks to yourself for the opportunity you have given yourself to learn and evolve.

13. Harm none as much as is humanly possible and do as you will. [254]

I, too, see these as being extremely important rules to live by.

Listen to your inner being.

Discover your reality from the *inside*, thereby directing your life in this way.

What gets very difficult, is allowing tyranny to take place, basically because emotions are involved.

Everyone is endowed with the potential to create their own reality, even if it does not mirror your own.

Most people on the planet, however, allow others to create and dictate their reality to them. In this manner, we have been encouraged to look outside of ourselves for the answers.

---

[254] Fraser, Ivan. "Love Changes Everything". The Truth Campaign magazine. September 2000: Volume 17, pages 50 and 51.

Vicarius Christi: The Vicar of Christ

As you begin to live according to your own guidance, daring to break free from the Matrix, everything changes; you become empowered when your emotions are no longer entangled with the Matrix that currently exists.

It is important to remember that in citing the Matrix, I am referring to those who create and dictate the reality for the multitude, the place from where darkness has been reigning.

It becomes my role to love and honor the Divine being that I am. Just as a wise parent must allow their child to grow through their own experiences, so, too, does the Creator allow us free will to evolve in this way.

I must resume, and assume, my own authority so as to lesson the complacency that currently exists on the planet. It becomes my role, therefore, to both trust my own identity as well as personal experiences with synchronicity.

In my desire to begin evolving, I made the conscious decision to become media free.

Vicarius Christi: The Vicar of Christ

I do not read the newspaper. I do not read news related magazines. I do not listen to the news on the radio. I do not watch the news on the television.

A process that spanned years, I knew this to be the only way for me to begin disengaging myself from the constant frequency of chaos, anxiety and stress that is prevalent on the planet.

I began to listen to what was going on inside of myself, living in the world, but yet not part of the emotional entanglement (which is where one can become hopelessly lost to the real Self).

Now that I have experienced considerable success in maintaining a significant level of neutrality, there are times when I may decide to re-inform myself as to worldly happenings.

Knowing that we are being controlled through our emotions, this is where the break must come. Maintaining neutrality is of extreme importance, as this is what serves to bring one to a place of empowerment.

Vicarius Christi: The Vicar of Christ

When you operate at a level of total sovereignty, those who wish to control you are not interested in you; they merely want a fearful, chaotic frequency, as this is what continues to give them power and control.

Fear and chaos "have predominated on this planet because these entities have stirred them up. They have divided and conquered everywhere to create that frequency. When you operate in peace and love and with information, you alter the structure of this place drastically: you bring choice of frequency back to this planet." [255]

Aside from religion and the media, the education system is another area where we are being controlled. The completion of my Masters program confirmed this on many levels. As an educator, this is something that I find myself wrestling with on a day-to-day basis.

It is becoming more and more imperative that we must learn to read energies, using more than our five senses to perceive reality, primarily because they merely serve to limit one's

---

[255] Marciniak, Barbara. (1992). *Bringers of the Dawn: Teachings from the Pleiadians* (page 96). Rochester, VT: Bear & Company Publishing.

perceptions of reality. Now is the time to begin relying on other forms of sensing, such as our knowing, intuitive, *feeling*, psychic self.

When one re-discovers their own way of intuiting, their own knowledge, they can no longer be controlled through fearful frequencies.

When a human being "broadcasts the frequency of fear, a transmission of consciousness is sent out. Where does that fear go? Where do your thoughts go? Where do your emotions go?" [256]

These are pertinent questions, to be sure. How many of us have ever really meditated, and deliberated, on the answers?

In awakening each morning, take the time to clearly state what you intend to experience throughout the day; herein lies the beginning to establishing your reality, for it is

---

[256] Marciniak, Barbara. (1992). *Bringers of the Dawn: Teachings from the Pleiadians* (page 113). Rochester, VT: Bear & Company Publishing.

thought that *creates experience* and *experience* that *creates reality*.

Your experience is *always* a direct reflection of what you are thinking. Your thoughts form your world *all* of the time.

As there exist so many frequency-control vibrations, you must remain clear and centered as to your thoughts, living in the now.

You are "a result of your thoughts. Thought creates experience. Why not give yourself a gift and begin to think of yourself in a capacity that is exceptional, magnificent, and uplifting." [257]

One's words can be either empowering or disempowering. It is important to eliminate the words *should* and *trying* from your vocabulary.

Should merely implies that you are operating under someone else's sovereignty. *Trying* does not mean the same as doing.

---

[257] Marciniak, Barbara. (1992). *Bringers of the Dawn: Teachings from the Pleiadians* (page 121). Rochester, VT: Bear & Company Publishing.

Vicarius Christi: The Vicar of Christ

Whenever you use the word *trying*, you will not accomplish anything because trying is an excuse.

Focus instead on these thoughts.

I am a *doer*.

I am a *manifestor*.

There is *no limitation* on this planet.

I am living my life in accordance with the light (which means that my frequency vibration is rising). In so doing, I am also altering the frequency of the planet.

There is nothing stronger "than your commitment to the exalted self. Once you commit yourself to the energy of light, the energy of exaltation, and uplifted frequency, you are marked." [258]

First and foremost, you must *live your light with courage*.

---

[258] Marciniak, Barbara. (1992). *Bringers of the Dawn: Teachings from the Pleiadians* (page 132). Rochester, VT: Bear & Company Publishing.

Vicarius Christi: The Vicar of Christ

You must also learn to *speak what you know without getting caught up in the drama.*

What does it mean to trust? It simply means "to have such inner knowing that your thoughts create your world; to simply be quite certain, with divine nonchalance and inner knowing, that *if you think something, it is.*" [259]

Information is light; light is information; hence, "the more you become informed, the more you alter your frequency. You are electromagnetic creatures, and everything that you are, you broadcast to someone else." [260]

I am here to evolve myself to the highest capability within this human form.

In so doing, I will also be affecting those around me in a positive way.

---

[259] Marciniak, Barbara. (1992). *Bringers of the Dawn: Teachings from the Pleiadians* (page 135). Rochester, VT: Bear & Company Publishing.
[260] Ibid, page 140.

Vicarius Christi: The Vicar of Christ

Once you can consistently maintain "a frequency of information and not be riding the roller coaster of emotions, up and down because you don't know who you are, you will be given a task. Your blueprint is your own personal detailed plan, or outline of action, for this lifetime." [261]

If you go into a meditative state, "you will receive a picture of your identity and reality and the next step of your assignment, day by day. Meditation is a way to get informed and to go to a place that nourishes you. You will move into your purpose and, more than likely, it will have to do with facilitating the frequency: transducing it, stepping it down to others, explaining it, using it to heal others, and stabilizing it for the human race. When each of you can hold a frequency of information without freaking out, and can be counted upon to be consistent, then you anchor the frequency on the planet. That frequency is recognized. It cannot be traced, exactly, but it can be recognized. That is why there has been a frenzied step-up to alter that frequency.

---

[261] Marciniak, Barbara. (1992). *Bringers of the Dawn: Teachings from the Pleiadians* (pages 140 to 141). Rochester, VT: Bear & Company Publishing.

You will see more frequency control everywhere you look, only now you will be able to recognize it for what it is." [262]

Stay focused on your own growth, your own path, your own self.

Do not overly concern yourself with what others are doing.

The female version of self is equated with intuition, receptivity, creativity, compassion, nourishment, whereas the male version of self is attributed with powerful, rational, intellectual.

You are looking for the *integration of the male and female essence* within yourself; this is what makes one whole.

We learn from experience, thereby arriving at a place where we truly value our uniqueness.

---

[262] Marciniak, Barbara. (1992). *Bringers of the Dawn: Teachings from the Pleiadians* (page 141). Rochester, VT: Bear & Company Publishing.

Vicarius Christi: The Vicar of Christ

The Hermit has long traveled the path, gaining wisdom and insight; standing alone, holding the lantern that reveals, most knowingly, that the answers sought, the higher calling and sense of purpose, lies within one's own soul.

The answers that we are looking for can never be found by looking outside of ourselves to other people, to other situations. Out of necessity, we must connect with our inner spirit, putting the conditioning of the outside world aside in order to figure out what we believe in, and what we choose to stand for.

It took some time for me to come to terms with the fact that focusing on one's personal needs is not being selfish.

How can one feel that they are an effective parent, spouse, teacher or friend, if they are not feeling secure and/or fulfilled within themselves?

It is also of the utmost importance that you never lose sight of your goals, always moving towards your highest aspirations. After all, one cannot exist indefinitely in the planning stages.

Growth requires action. In this light, it is important to do whatever it takes to maintain one's enthusasm in order to remain true to their purpose.

When we are truly passionate about a goal, the energy to achieve it will follow.

That being said, it is also important to acknowledge that one's choices often have long-term, and even lifetime, rewards and/or consequences; hence, it is important to make balanced decisions by way of careful considerations.

Knowledge is power. It is important, therefore, to educate oneself on a continuous basis, refusing to meekly accept that which is spoon fed to the multitude.

When one is on a quest for truth, it is always important to look below the surface. Important decisions are made with enhanced clarity when one is able to distance themselves from drama, using strategy as opposed to reacting to events.

In making happiness and peace a conscious choice, such is where your true power lies.

Vicarius Christi: The Vicar of Christ

Read with discernment.

It is important to come at things from many different angles.

See what resonates with you, what feels right. It is up to each to decide what to do with the information; each individual is in charge of their own life.

Find what it is that you know, not what you want to believe or what you have been told.

Trusting what you know is imperative.

When you trust what you know, you are activating that part of you that is connected to the Creator.

It is high time that we come back to that intuitive side of ourselves, a side that has long been forgotten due to the emphasis placed solely on the logical.

All we need to know resides within. We have but to remember. So, too, does this involve releasing ourselves from the ego trappings of the physical.

Vicarius Christi: The Vicar of Christ

In making personal choices, I am responsible for my actions. I am also learning the importance of choosing to work for the highest good of the whole, and yet there also comes the responsibility of realizing that one must avoid infringing upon the rights of another.

In reference to the accessing of knowledge, "it used to be that each individual who evolved and studied the mysteries had one teacher, and knowledge was passed down from teacher to apprentice, in a long line of tradition." [263]

Today, however, "you become your own teacher by activating what is inside you, through *clear intent*, and by following the impulses and knowledge that accompany the process." [264]

The inner you communicates, on a continuous basis, "with a you that can be called your higher self, or your inner teacher. It is a version of you, invisible to your current perceptions, that nonetheless has a powerful influence. Your higher self

---

[263] Marciniak, Barbara. (1994). *Earth: Pleiadian Keys to the Living Library* (page 55). Rochester, VT: Bear & Company Publishing.
[264] Ibid, page 33.

Vicarius Christi: The Vicar of Christ

is connected with a vista of reality in which there is a purpose to all you select to experience. Ideally, your higher self communicates this grander view to you by way of impulse, synchronicity, and emotion. It is up to *you* to translate your own messages and realize that, as you decree, reality conforms." [265]

The training that you are receiving "is from your inner teacher. You have a blueprint inside you that leads to a different pathway. You learn by following what is awakening from within. You will gain the greatest amount of knowledge through personal experience. Acknowledge that there is something for you to learn in every event you encounter in your life." [266]

It is my belief that all of humanity is here to learn an important lesson; the realization that we are connected to all that exists.

---

[265] Marciniak, Barbara. (1994). *Earth: Pleiadian Keys to the Living Library* (page 68). Rochester, VT: Bear & Company Publishing.
[266] Ibid, page 72.

Vicarius Christi: The Vicar of Christ

We are magnificent beings.

Remembering who we are will help to bring about the changes that are needed.

Mind you, in order to do so, we have to get out of our own way.

Many are currently moving along the path towards Ascension, moving to a higher vibrational level that is also associated with the Christ Consciousness.

This is a level of awareness that "does not judge, does not criticize, coerce, tempt, does not condone, does not react negatively" for Christ Consciousness is "true wisdom, Divine truth, true happiness, unconditional love and total perfection." [267]

Mastering the ego is key, but seeing and feeling only the beauty that exists, within the moment, is paramount.

---

[267] Crea. What is Christ Consciousness. Retrieved March 9, 2008, from http://www.lightascension.com/arts/christconsciousness.htm

Vicarius Christi: The Vicar of Christ

Having recently received information on two videos of significant importance ……

[1] *We Are All One Consciousness* [268]

[2] *Even The Troops Are Waking Up* [269]

…… clearly, we are all *one consciousness* experiencing itself subjectively. In the course of your individual journey, it is my wish that you, too, will be able to arrive at the same conclusion.

It is also my belief that our bodies are sacred temples dedicated to God(dess). In the uniting of body, mind and soul, you have the power to prevent negative thoughts and feelings from desecrating your temple. In the uniting of body, mind and soul, thereby living the dictates of a heart-based consciousness, so, too, do you have the power to release the anger, the hostility, and the frustration, that may be residing within your being.

---

[268] http://www.davidicke.com/articles/media-and-appearances/36572-we-are-all-one-consciousness-human-race-get-off-your-knees

[269] http://www.davidicke.com/articles/media-and-appearances/36265-even-the-troops-are-waking-up-a-fantastic-video

Vicarius Christi: The Vicar of Christ

As a result, I am able to access, honor, acknowledge and recognize God(dess) every minute of every day.

It is my belief that we are here to embrace (and live) love and compassion. We are not here to be chained to the distorted messages of fear, guilt, prejudice and bigotry.

You do not "have to have a relationship with people who cause you disharmony and who are affecting the peace and serenity of your soul." [270] You can feel free to respond, with unconditional love, at a safe distance, via telephone, snail mail and/or email.

You are here to *remain true to yourself*. As you take the time to nurture your own spirit and soul, you become a manifestation of God(dess).

Learn how to "express love to others. Let others feel your love by your words, your body language, your attitude, the look in your eyes, your behavior, and your actions. Not only will you touch the lives of thousands of people, but you,

---

[270] Bunick, Nick. (1998) *In God's Truth* (page 175). Charlottesville, VA: Hampton Roads Publishing Corporation, Inc.

yourself, will feel a greater joy and harmony inside of you than you have ever felt before." [271]

You do not require any help outside of yourself to evolve spiritually; everything you need can be found within.

Take the time to get to know who you really are.

Seek (knowledge) *and ye shall find* (knowledge) for it is positive energy that nourishes the soul and truth that liberates.

Although it is back to the classroom for me, to learn how best to reach that place within that is unconditioned and formless (spirit), inviting stillness into my life, I trust that I will have provided you, the reader, with a sense of direction that you may be able to follow.

---

[271] Bunick, Nick. (1998) *In God's Truth* (page 180). Charlottesville, VA: Hampton Roads Publishing Corporation, Inc.

Context for Today

The Gnostics placed an emphasis on [1] spiritual knowledge (gnosis) as compared to faith; a self-knowledge obtained through understanding, courtesy of an inner, mystical (esoteric) and [2] contemplative experience (whereby one acquires knowledge of, and acquaintance with, the divine), coupled with [3] purified living (conscious living) in keeping with all life.

This knowledge, this realization, is experiential, meaning that it can never be attained through reason because it has no basis in intellectualism.

As multi-dimensional beings, we have never been souls that were lost, we have never been souls that were diseased, we have never been souls that needed to be saved; however, we *did* come to experience ourselves in all ways, these included, as a means of evolutionary development from a spiritual perspective.

There exists a higher, cosmic, consciousness that we are here to achieve.

Yogis call it super consciousness; Gurdjieff references it as objective consciousness; Theosophists cite it as Buddhic consciousness; Sufism and Hinduism expresses the same as God consciousness; New Agers state it as Christ consciousness. [272]

In essence, each expression is used to denote the consciousness of a human being who has reached a higher level of evolutionary development, in that he/she has come to know, and understand, reality versus illusion.

Within a secular context, "higher consciousness is usually associated with exceptional control over one's mind and will, intellectual and moral enlightenment, and profound personal growth" [273] whereas in a primarily spiritual context, higher consciousness may "also be associated with transcendence, spiritual enlightenment, and union with the divine." [274]

---

[272] http://en.wikipedia.org/wiki/Higher_consciousness
[273] Ibid.
[274] Ibid.

Vicarius Christi: The Vicar of Christ

What makes consciousness so intriguing is that most humans are considered to be asleep (to both the reality versus the illusion equation as well as the infinite versus the finite statement) even as they go about their daily business. This is why movies such as *The Peaceful Warrior* and *The Matrix* series are so important.

Many attribute the Golden Rule (meaning, do unto others as you would have them do unto you) to Jesus, as author. Ancient books from China, however, document the sage Meng-tse (370 BCE), whose name was Latinized to Mencius, the pupil of Confucius, as the composer. [275]

There is a Masonic principle, called *acting on the square*, a familiar metaphor for fair and honest dealings with others, that dates back to ancient China; a principle that references that an individual should abstain from doing to another that which he would not want done unto himself. [276] [277]

---

[275] Vayro, Ian Ross. (2007) *God Save Us From Religion* (page 115). Queensland, Australia: Joshua Books.
[276] Ibid.

Vicarius Christi: The Vicar of Christ

Such is further attributed to a book called The Great Learning (written in 500 BC). [278] [279] [280]

In truth, a person can only become informed and enlightened if *they are open to new possibilities*. You must be willing to let go in order to grow into what it means to be empowered.

What is truly interesting is that the Bible denotes the following: [1] *Ye shall be as Gods* (Genesis 3:5), [2] *Behold, the man is become as one of us* (Genesis 3:22) and [3] *You, too, are Gods* (Psalm 82). [281]

Truly, this is in keeping with "the perennial mysticism of Gnosticism and the Pagan mysteries – that within each one

---

[277] http://www.themasonictrowel.com/Articles/degrees/degree_3rd_files/the_square_gltx.htm
[278] http://www.sacred-texts.com/cfu/menc/
[279] http://www.sacred-texts.com/mas/syma/syma34.htm
[280] http://www.indiana.edu/~p374/Daxue.pdf
[281] Vayro, Ian Ross. (2006) *They Lied To Us in Sunday School* (page 377). Queensland, Australia: Joshua Books.

Vicarius Christi: The Vicar of Christ

of us is the one Soul of the Universe, the Logos, the Universal Daemon, the Mind of God." [282]

Aside from delving within, there is no need to seek. In essence, the purpose of our evolutionary pilgrimage is "to bring this inner Christ or Buddha nature to full expression over the course of numberless lives." [283]

In the words of Eckhart Tolle ... *You are not in the now, you are the now; that is your essential identity: the only thing that never changes. Life is always now. Now is consciousness and consciousness is who you are. That's the equation.*

In the words of Lama Surya Das ... *Enlightenment is not about becoming divine. Instead, it's about becoming more fully human. It is the end of ignorance.*

---

[282] Freke, Timothy and Gandy, Peter. (1999) *The Jesus Mysteries* (page 46). New York, New York: Three Rivers Press.
[283] http://davidpratt.info/jesus.htm

Vicarius Christi: The Vicar of Christ

Advaita Meetup Groups [284]

Adyashanti [285]

Adyashanti: A Matter of Perspective [286]

Alan Watts: An Interactive Experience [287]

An Introduction to Awareness [288]

Authenticity Accelerator (Robert Rabbin) [289]

Being Yoga [290]

Charlie Todd: The Shared Experience of Absurdity [291]

---

[284] http://advaita.meetup.com/
[285] http://www.adyashanti.org/
[286] http://vimeo.com/21318776
[287] http://alanwatts.com/archive/
[288] http://www.anintroductiontoawareness.com/Awareness/Introduction.html
[289] http://authenticityaccelerator.com/
[290] http://www.beingyoga.com/
[291] http://www.ted.com/talks/charlie_todd_the_shared_experience_of_absurdity.html?utm_source=newsletter_weekly_2011-11-11

Vicarius Christi: The Vicar of Christ

Daily Zen Meditation [292]

Dharma Tunes [293]

Die to Love [294]

Free Awareness [295]

Free Hugs (Juan Mann) [296]

Free Hugs Campaign [297]

Free Hugs Message from Juan Mann [298]

Inviting Awareness [299]

Jerry Katz: On the Ever-Expanding World of Nonduality [300]

---

[292] http://www.dailyzen.com/meditation.asp
[293] http://dharmatunes.com/
[294] http://not-knowing.com/
[295] http://www.free-awareness.com/
[296] http://www.youtube.com/watch?v=vr3x_RRJdd4
[297] http://www.juanmann.com/
[298] http://www.youtube.com/watch?v=BRVzXcybd2c&feature=relmfu
[299] http://canelamichelle.com/
[300] http://nondualityamerica.wordpress.com/2011/07/23/jerry-katz-on-the-ever-expanding-world-of-nonduality/

Vicarius Christi: The Vicar of Christ

Living As the Source of Who You Are [301]

Living Realization [302]

Natural Awakening [303]

Never Not Here [304]

Nondualism Meetup Groups [305]

Nonduality Activism (Jerry Katz) [306]

Nonduality Meetup Groups [307]

Nonduality Satsang Nova Scotia (Jerry Katz) [308]

Non-Duality America Blog [309]

---

[301] http://chuckhillig.com/Home_Page.html
[302] http://livingrealization.org/
[303] http://www.nondualtraining.com/
[304] http://www.nevernothere.com/
[305] http://nondualism.meetup.com/
[306] http://nonduality.com/activism.htm
[307] http://nonduality.meetup.com/
[308] http://www.nonduality.ca/
[309] http://nondualityamerica.wordpress.com/author/nondualityamercia/

Non-Duality Magazine [310]

No Shame in Stillness [311]

Nothing Exists, Despite Appearances [312]

Nothing Saying This: Nonduality Blog [313]

Please Respect My Religion [314]

Radiance of Being [315]

Radiant Mind [316]

Science and Non-Duality [317]

---

[310] http://www.nondualitymagazine.org/nonduality_magazine.contents.volume.5.htm
[311] http://undertheapricottree.wordpress.com/2011/10/18/no-shame-in-stillness/
[312] http://nothingexistsdespiteappearances.blogspot.com/
[313] http://nothingsayingthis.com/
[314] http://freethoughtnation.com/contributing-writers/63-acharya-s/614-please-respect-my-religion.html
[315] http://radianceofbeing.blogspot.com/
[316] http://www.radiantmind.net/
[317] http://www.scienceandnonduality.com/

Vicarius Christi: The Vicar of Christ

Scott Morrison Teachings [318]

Stillness Speaks [319]

The Benefits of Mystical Oneness [320]

The Bhagavan Sri Ramana Maharshi website [321]

The Birth and Death of Fundamentalism in Nonduality and Advaita Teachings [322]

The Church of Reality [323]

The Illustrated Guide to Free Hugs (Juan Mann) [324]

The Rambling Taoists [325]

---

[318] http://scotmorrison.wordpress.com/
[319] http://chucksurface.stillnessspeaks.com/
[320] http://waynewirs.com/the-benefits-of-mystical-oneness/
[321] http://www.sriramanamaharshi.org/
[322] http://www.lifewithoutacentre.com/read/essays-transcripts/the-birth-and-death-of-fundamentalism-in-nonduality-and-advaita-teachings/
[323] http://www.churchofreality.org/wisdom/hidden_agenda/
[324] https://www.createspace.com/3447347
[325] http://ramblingtaoist.blogspot.com/2011/12/hsin-hsin-ming-viii-non-duality.html

Vicarius Christi: The Vicar of Christ

The Rambling Taoists Miscellaneous Writings [326]

The Spiritual Mind [327]

Undivided: The Online Journal of Nonduality and Psychology [328]

Urban Guru Magazine [329]

Vicki Woodyard [330]

Wake Up [331]

---

[326] http://ramblingtaoist.wordpress.com/scott-bradley/miscellaneous-writings/
[327] http://thespiritualmind-holly.blogspot.com/
[328] http://undividedjournal.com/
[329] http://urbangurumagazine.com/
[330] http://www.nondualitynow.com/
[331] http://wakeupthefilm.com/

Bibliography

CATHARISM

Arnold, John. (2001) *Inquisition and Power: Catharism and the Confessing Subject in Medieval Languedoc.*

Barber, Malcolm. (2000) *The Cathars: Dualist Heretics in Languedoc in the High Middle Ages.*

Burnham, Sophy. (2002) *The Treasure of Montségur: A Novel of the Cathars.*

Costen, Michael. (1997) *The Cathars and The Albigensian Crusade.*

Cowper, Marcus and Dennis, Peter. (2006) *Cathar Castles: Fortresses of the Albigensian Crusade 1209-1300.*

Craney, Glen. (2008) *The Fire and the Light: A Novel of the Cathars and the Lost Teachings of Christ.*

Douzet, André. (2006) *The Wandering of the Grail: The Cathars, the Search for the Grail, and the Discovery of Egyptian Relics in the French Pyrenees.*

Guirdham, Arthur. (2004) *The Cathars & Reincarnation.*

Guirdham, Arthur. (2004) *We Are One Another.*

Guirdham, Arthur. (2004) *The Lake and The Castle.*

Hughes, Nita. (2003) *Past Recall: When Love and Wisdom Transcend Time.*

Hughes, Nita. (2006) *The Cathar Legacy.*

Lambert, Malcolm D. (1998) *The Cathars.*

Markale, Jean. (2003) *Montségur and The Mystery of the Cathars.*

Martin, Sean. (2004) *The Cathars: The Most Successful Heresy of the Middle Ages.*

Mattingly, Alan. (2005) *Walking in the Cathar Region: Cathar Castles of South West France.*

Moerland, Bram. (2009) *The Cathars*.

O'Shea, Stephen (2001) *The Perfect Heresy: The Revolutionary Life and Death of the Medieval Cathars*.

Stoyanov, Yuri. (2000) *The Other God: Dualist Religions from Antiquity to the Cathar Heresy*.

Strayer, Joseph. (1992) *The Albigensian Crusades*.

Vasilev, Georgi. (2007) *Heresy and the English Reformation: Bogomil-Cathar Influence on Wycliffe, Langland, Tyndale and Milton*.

Weis, Rene. (2002) *The Yellow Cross: The Story of the Last Cathar's Rebellion Against the Inquisition, 1290-1329*.

EGYPTIAN CONNECTIONS

Ashton, John, and Down, David. (2006) *Unwrapping the Pharaohs: How Egyptian Archaeology Confirms The Biblical Timeline*.

Ellis, Ralph. (2002) *Jesus: Last of the Pharaohs*.

Ellis, Ralph. (2002) *Tempest and Exodus*.

Ellis, Ralph. (2003) *Solomon: Falcon of Sheba: The Tomb and Image of the Queen of Sheba Discovered.*

Ellis, Ralph. (2006) *Cleopatra to Christ: Jesus Was The Great Grandson Of Cleopatra / Scota: Egyptian Queen Of The Scots.*

Ellis, Ralph. (2008) *Eden in Egypt: Adam and Eve were Pharaoh Akhenaten and Queen Nefertiti.*

Ellis, Ralph. (2008) *King Jesus: From Kam (Egypt) To Camelot.*

Harpur, Tom. (2005) *The Pagan Christ: Recovering the Lost Light.*

Murdock, D. M. (2009). *Christ in Egypt: The Horus-Jesus Connection.*

Osman, Ahmed. (2002) *Moses and Akhenaten: The Secret History of Egypt at the Time of the Exodus.*

Osman, Ahmed. (2003) *The Hebrew Pharaohs of Egypt: The Secret Lineage of the Patriarch Joseph.*

Osman, Ahmed. (2004) *Jesus in the House of the Pharaohs: The Essene Revelations on the Historical Jesus.*

Osman, Ahmed. (2005) *Christianity: An Ancient Egyptian Religion.*

HOLY BLOODLINE, HOLY GRAIL

Andrews, Richard. (1996) *The Tomb of God: The Body of Jesus and The Solution To A 2,000 Year Old Mystery.*

Arimathea, Joseph of. (1999) *The Book of The Holy Grail.*

Baigent, Michael; Leigh, Richard and Lincoln, Henry. (2004) *Holy Blood, Holy Grail.*

Bradley, Michael. (1996) *Holy Grail Across the Atlantic: The Secret History of Canadian Discovery and Exploration.*

Bradley, Michael. (1998) *Grail Knights of North America: On the Trail of the Grail Legacy in Canada and the United States.*

Bradley, Michael. (2005) *Swords at Sunset: Last Stand of North America's Grail Knights.*

Emerys, Chevalier. (2007) *Revelation of the Holy Grail*.

Francke, Sylvia. (2007) *The Tree of Life and The Holy Grail: Ancient and Modern Spiritual Paths and the Mystery of Rennes-le-Château*.

Gardiner, Philip and Osborn, Gary. (2006) *The Serpent Grail: The Truth Behind the Holy Grail, the Philosopher's Stone and the Elixir of Life*.

Gardner, Laurence. (2000) *Genesis of the Grail Kings: The Explosive Story of Genetic Cloning of and the Ancient Bloodline of Jesus*.

Gardner, Laurence. (2001) *Bloodline of the Holy Grail: The Hidden Lineage of Jesus Revealed*.

Gardner, Laurence. (2006) *The Magdalene Legacy: The Jesus and Mary Bloodline Conspiracy*.

Gardner, Laurence. (2008) *The Grail Enigma: The Hidden Heirs of Jesus and Mary Magdalene*.

Johnson, Bettye. (2005) *Secrets of the Magdalene Scrolls: The Forbidden Truth of the Life and Times of Mary Magdalene.*

Johnson, Bettye. (2007) *Mary Magdalene, Her Story.*

Lincoln, Henry. (2004) *The Holy Place: Sauniere and the Decoding of the Mystery of Rennes-le-Château.*

Miles, Rosalind. (2002) *The Child of the Holy Grail.*

Montgomery, Hugh. (2006) *The God-Kings of Europe: The Descendants of Jesus Traced Through the Odonic and Davidic Dynasties.*

Montgomery, Hugh. (2007) *The God-Kings of England: The Viking and Norman Dynasties and their Conquest of England (983 to 1066).*

Montgomery, Hugh. (2008) *The God-Kings of Outremer.*

Montgomery, Hugh. (2010) *The God-Kings of the Vikings: The Viking Dynasties and their Conquests of Northern Europe (850 to 1086).*

Ortenberg, Veronica. (2006) *In Search of The Holy Grail*.

Phillips, Graham. (2001) *The Marian Conspiracy: The Hidden Truth About the Holy Grail, The Real Father of Christ*.

Pinkham, Mark Amaru. (2004) *Guardians of the Holy Grail: The Knights Templar, John the Baptist, and the Water of Life*.

Simmans, Graham. (2007) *Jesus After The Crucifixion: From Jerusalem to Rennes-le-Château*.

Twyman, Tracy R. (2004) *The Merovingian Mythos and the Mystery of Rennes-le-Château*.

Wallace-Murphy, Tim and Hopkins, Marilyn. (2000) *Rosslyn: Guardian of the Secret of the Holy Grail*.

Wallace-Murphy, Tim; Simmons, Graham and Hopkins, Marilyn. (2000) *Rex Deus: The True Mystery of Rennes-le-Château*.

Young, John K. (2003) *Sacred Sites of the Knights Templar: Ancient Astronomers and Freemasons at Stonehenge, Rennes-le-Château and Santiago de Compostela.*

KNIGHTS TEMPLAR

Addison, Charles G. (1997) *History of the Knights Templar.*

Barber, Malcolm. (1993) *The Trial of the Templars.*

Bradley, Michael. (1996) *Holy Grail Across the Atlantic: The Secret History of Canadian Discovery and Exploration.*

Bradley, Michael. (1998) *Grail Knights of North America: On the Trail of the Grail Legacy in Canada and the United States.*

Bradley, Michael. (2005) *Swords at Sunset: Last Stand of North America's Grail Knights.*

Bradley, Michael. (2008) *The Secrets about the Freemasons.*

Butler, Alan and Dafoe, Stephen. (1999) *The Knights Templar Revealed: The Secrets of the Cistercian Legacy.*

Butler, Alan and Dafoe, Stephen. (2006) *The Warriors and the Bankers: A History of the Knights Templar from 1307 to the Present.*

Dafoe, Stephen. (2007) *Nobly Born: An Illustrated History of The Knights Templar.*

Dafoe, Stephen. (2008) *The Compass and the Cross: A History of the Masonic Knights Templar.*

Gardner, Laurence. (2007) *The Shadow of Solomon: The Lost Secret of the Freemasons Revealed.*

Knight, Christopher and Lomas, Robert. (2001) *The Hiram Key: Pharaohs, Freemasonry, and the Discovery of the Secret Scrolls of Jesus.*

Knight, Christopher and Lomas, Robert. (2001) *Second Messiah: Templars, the Turin Shroud and the Great Secret of Freemasonry.*

Mann, William. (2004) *The Knights Templar in the New World: How Henry Sinclair Brought the Grail to Acadia.*

Mann, William. (2006) *The Templar Meridians: The Secret Mapping of the New World.*

Picknett, Lynn and Prince, Clive. (1998) *The Templar Revelation: Secret Guardians of the True Identity of Christ.*

Picknett, Lynn and Prince, Clive. (2007) *The Turin Shroud: How Da Vinci Fooled History.*

Pinkham, Mark Amaru. (2004) *Guardians of the Holy Grail: The Knights Templar, John the Baptist, and the Water of Life.*

Read, Paul Piers. (1999) *The Templars.*

Robinson, John J. (1991) *Dungeon, Fire and Sword.*

Sora, Steven. (1999) *The Lost Treasure of the Knights Templar: Solving the Oak Island Mystery.*

Sora, Steven. (2004) *Lost Colony of the Templars: Verrazano's Secret Mission to America.*

Wallace-Murphy, Tim and Hopkins, Marilyn. (2007) *Templars in America.*

Wallace-Murphy, Tim. (2008) *The Knights of the Holy Grail: The Secret History of the Knights Templar*.

Young, John K. (2003) *Sacred Sites of the Knights Templar: Ancient Astronomers and Freemasons at Stonehenge, Rennes-le-Château and Santiago de Compostela*.

MEROVINGIANS

Baird, Robert Bruce. (2008) *Merovingians: Past and Present Masters*.

Gardner, Laurence. (2003) *Realm of the Ring Lords: The Myth and Magic of the Grail Quest*.

Geary, Patrick J. (1994) *Before France and Germany: The Creation and Transformation of the Merovingian World*.

Murray, Alexander Callander. (2000) *From Roman to Merovingian Gaul: A Reader*.

Murray, Alexander Callander. (2005) *Gregory of Tours: The Merovingians*.

Wallace-Hadrill, J. M. (1982) *The Long-Haired Kings and Other Studies in Frankish History*.

Wood, I. (1995) *The Merovingian Kingdoms, 450-751*.

TRUTH AND HIGHER CONSCIOUSNESS

Ambrose, Kala. (2007) *9 Life Altering Lessons: Secrets of the Mystery Schools Unveiled*.

Braden, Gregg. (1995) *Awakening to Zero Point: The Collective Initiation*.

Braden, Gregg. (1997) *Walking Between the Worlds: The Science of Compassion*.

Braden, Gregg. (2000) *The Isaiah Effect: Decoding the Lost Science of Prayer and Prophecy*.

Braden, Gregg. (2000) *Beyond Zero Point: The Journey to Compassion*.

Braden, Gregg, (2004) *The God Code: The Secret of Our Past, The Promise of Our Future*.

Braden, Gregg. (2004) *The Divine Name: Sounds of the God Code* (audio book).

Braden, Gregg. (2005) *The Lost Mode of Prayer* (audio CD).

Braden, Gregg. (2005) *Unleashing The Power of The God Code: The Mystery and Meaning of the Message in Our Cells* (audio CD).

Braden, Gregg. (2005) *An Ancient Magical Prayer: Insights from the Dead Sea Scrolls* (audio book).

Braden, Gregg. (2005) *Speaking the Lost Language of God: Awakening the Forgotten Wisdom of Prayer, Prophecy and the Dead Sea Scrolls* (audio book).

Braden, Gregg. (2005) *Awakening the Power of A Modern God: Unlock the Mystery and Healing of Your Spiritual DNA* (audio book).

Braden, Gregg. (2006) *Secrets of The Lost Mode of Prayer*.

Braden, Gregg. (2007) *The Divine Matrix: Bridging Time, Space, Miracles and Belief.*

Bunick, Nick. (1998) *In God's Truth*.

Bunick, Nick. (2011) *Time for Truth: A New Beginning*.

Bunick, Nick. (2011) *The Commitment*.

Bunick, Nick. (2011) *The Messengers: Fourteen Years Later*.

Bushby, Tony. (2001) *The Bible Fraud: The Untold Story of Jesus Christ*.

Bushby, Tony. (2003) *The Secret in The Bible*.

Bushby, Tony. (2004) *The Crucifixion of Truth*.

Bushby, Tony. (2005) *The Twin Deception*.

Bushby, Tony. (2007) *The Papal Billions*.

Bushby, Tony. (2008) *The Christ Scandal*.

Chopra, Deepak. (1998) *The Path to Love: Spiritual Strategies for Healing*.

Chopra, Deepak. (2005) *Peace Is The Way: Bringing War and Violence to An End.*

Coelho, Paulo. (1998) *The Alchemist.*

Coelho, Paulo. (2003) *Warrior Of The Light.*

Crowley, Gary. (2006) *From Here to Here: Turning Toward Enlightenment.*

Das, Lama Surys. (1998) *Awakening the Buddha Within.*

Das, Lama Surys. (2000) *Awakening to the Sacred: Creating a Spiritual Life From Scratch.*

Das, Lama Surys. (2001) *Awakening the Buddhist Heart: Integrating Love, Meaning and Connection Into Every Part of Your Life.*

Das, Lama Surys. (2003) *Living Kindness: The Buddha's Ten Guiding Principles for a Blessed Life.*

Das, Lama Surys. (2003) *Letting Go of the Person You Used To Be: Lessons on Change, Loss and Spiritual Transformation.*

Doucette, Michele. (2010) *A Travel in Time to Grand Pré* (second edition).

Doucette, Michele. (2010) *The Ultimate Enlightenment For 2012: All We Need Is Ourselves*.

Doucette, Michele. (2010) *Turn Off The TV: Turn On Your Mind*.

Doucette, Michele. (2010) *Veracity At Its Best*.

Doucette, Michele. (2010) *The Collective: Essays on Reality*.

Doucette, Michele. (2011) *Sleepers Awaken: The Time Is Now To Consciously Create Your Own Reality*.

Doucette, Michele. (2011) *Healing the Planet and Ourselves: How To Raise Your Vibration*.

Doucette, Michele. (2011) *You Are Everything: Everything Is You*.

Doucette, Michele. (2011) *The Awakening of Humanity: A Foremost Necessity*.

Doucette, Michele. (2011) *The Cosmos of The Soul: A Spiritual Biography*.

Doucette, Michele. (2011) *Getting Out Of Our Own Way: Love Is The Only Answer*.

Doucette, Michele. (2011) *Back Home With Evangeline*.

Doucette, Michele. (2012) *Living the Jedi Way*.

Dyer, Wayne. (1998) *Manifest Your Destiny: The Nine Spiritual Principles For Getting Everything That You Want*.

Dyer, Wayne. (2002) *Getting in the Gap: Making Conscious Contact with God Through Meditation* (book and CD).

Flavius Philostratus. *The Life of Apollonius of Tyana*.

Ford. (2005) *Becoming God*.

Ford, Debbie. (2010) *The 21 Day Consciousness Cleanse: A Breakthrough Program for Connecting with Your Soul's Deepest Purpose*.

Freke, Timothy. (2005) *Lucid Living*.

Freke, Timothy. (2009) *How Long Is Now? A Journey to Enlightenment and Beyond.*

Freke, Timothy, and Gandy, Peter. (2001) *The Jesus Mysteries: Was the Original Jesus a Pagan God?*

Freke, Timothy, and Gandy, Peter. (2002) *Jesus and The Lost Goddess: The Secret Teachings of the Original Christians.*

Freke, Timothy, and Gandy, Peter. (2006) *The Laughing Jesus: Religious Lies and Gnostic Wisdom.*

Freke, Timothy, and Gandy, Peter. (2007) *The Gospel of the Second Coming.*

Gawain, Shakti. (1993) *Living In The Light: A Guide to Personal and Planetary Transformation.*

Gawain, Shakti. (1999) *The Four Levels of Healing.*

Gawain, Shakti. (2000) *The Path of Transformation: How Healing Ourselves Can Change The World.*

Gawain, Shakti. (2003) *Reflections in The Light: Daily Thoughts and Affirmations*.

Hansard, Christopher. (2003) *The Tibetan Art of Positive Thinking*.

Hicks, Esther and Hicks, Jerry. (2004) *Ask and It Is Given: Learning to Manifest Your Desires*.

Hicks, Esther and Hicks, Jerry. (2005) *The Amazing Power of Deliberate Intent: Living the Art of Allowing*.

Hicks, Esther and Hicks, Jerry. (2006) *The Law of Attraction: The Basics of the Teachings of Abraham*.

Hicks, Esther and Hicks, Jerry. (2008) *The Astonishing Power of Emotions: Let Your Feelings Be Your Guide*.

Hicks, Esther and Hicks, Jerry. (2009) *The Vortex: Where The Law of Attraction Assembles all Cooperative Relationships*.

James, John. (2007) *The Great Field: Soul At Play In The Conscious Universe*.

Johnson, Bettye. (2011) *What The Blank Do We Know About The Bible?* free downloadable ebook [332]

Judd, Isha. (2008) *Why Walk When You Can Fly: Soar Beyond Your Fears and Love Yourself and Others Unconditionally.*

Katz, Jerry. (2007) *One: Essential Writings on Nonduality.*

Koven, Jean-Claude. (2004) *Going Deeper: How To Make Sense of Your Life When Your Life Makes No Sense.*

Kribbe, Pamela. (2008) *The Jeshua Channelings: Christ Consciousness in a New Era.*

Lama, Dalai. (2004) *The Wisdom of Forgiveness: Intimate Conversations and Journey.*

McTaggart, Lynne. (2003) *The Field: The Quest For The Secret Force Of The Universe.*

McTaggart, Lynne. (2008) *The Intention Experiment: Using Your Thoughts to Change Your Life and the World.*

---

[332] http://www.magdalenescrolls.com/Product_Details_8.htm

McTaggart, Lynne. (2011) *The Bond: Connecting Through the Space Between Us*.

Millman, Dan. (1990) *Way of the Peaceful Warrior*.

Millman, Dan. (1991) *Sacred Journey of the Peaceful Warrior*.

Millman, Dan. (1992) *No Ordinary Moments: A Peaceful Warrior's Guide to Daily Life*.

Millman, Dan. (1995) *The Life You Were Born To Live*.

Millman, Dan. (1999) *Everyday Enlightenment*.

Moses, Jeffrey. (2002) *Oneness: Great Principles Shared By All Religions*.

Murdock, D. M. (2009). *The Gospel According To Acharya S*.

Nichols, L. Joseph (2000) *The Soul As Healer: Lessons in Affirmation, Visualization and Inner Power*.

Peniel, Jon. (1998) *The Lost Teachings of Atlantis: The Children of The Law of One*.

Peniel, Jon. (1999) *The Golden Rule Workbook: A Manual for the New Millennium.*

Price, John Randolph. (1987) *The Superbeings.*

Price, John Randolph. (1998) *The Success Book.*

Quinn, Gary. (2003) *Experience Your Greatness: Give Yourself Permission To Live* (audio CD).

Radin, Dean I. (2006) *Entangled Minds: Extrasensory Experiences in a Quantum Reality.*

Radin, Dean I. (2009) *The Conscious Universe: The Scientific Truth of Psychic Phenomena.*

Redfield, James. (1995) *The Celestine Prophecy.*

Redfield, James. (1997) *The Celestine Vision: Living the New Spiritual Awareness.*

Redfield, James. (1998) *The Tenth Insight.*

Redfield, James. (1999) *The Secret of Shambhala.*

Renard, Gary. (2004) *The Disappearance of the Universe.*

Renard, Gary. (2006) *Your Immortal Reality: How To Break the Cycle of Birth and Death.*

Rennison, Susan Joy. (2008) *Tuning the Diamonds: Electromagnetism and Spiritual Evolution.*

Ruiz, Don Miguel. (1997) *The Four Agreements: A Practical Guide to Personal Freedom.*

Ruiz, Don Miguel. (1999) *The Mastery of Love: A Practical Guide to The Art of Relationship.*

Ruiz, Don Miguel. (2000) *The Four Agreements Companion Book.*

Ruiz, Don Miguel. (2004) *The Voice of Knowledge: A Practical Guide to Inner Peace.*

Ruiz, Don Miguel. (2009) *Fifth Agreement: A Practical Guide to Self-Mastery.*

Schuman, Helen. (1997) *A Course in Miracles.*

Schwartz, Robert. (2009) *Your Soul's Plan: Discovering the Real Meaning of the Life You Planned Before You Were Born.*

Sharma, Robin. (1997) *The Monk Who Sold His Ferrari.*

Sharma, Robin. (2005) *Big Ideas to Live Your Best Life: Discover Your Destiny.*

Shinn, Florence Scovel. (1989) *The Wisdom of Florence Scovel Shinn.*

Shinn, Florence Scovel. (1991) *The Game of Life Affirmation and Inspiration Cards: Positive Words For A Positive Life.*

Shinn, Florence Scovel. (2006) *The Game of Life* (book and CD).

Talbot, Michael. (1992) *The Holographic Universe.*

Talbot, Michael. (1993) *Mysticism and the New Physics.*

Tolle, Eckhart. (1999) *The Power of Now: A Guide to Spiritual Enlightenment.*

Tolle, Eckhart. (2001) *Practicing the Power of Now: Meditations, Exercises and Core Teachings for Living the Liberated Life.*

Tolle, Eckhart. (2001) *The Realization of Being: A Guide to Experiencing Your True Identity* (audio CD).

Tolle, Eckhart. (2003) *Stillness Speaks.*

Tolle, Eckhart. (2003) *Entering The Now* (audio CD).

Tolle, Eckhart. (2005) *A New Earth: Awakening to Your Life's Purpose.*

Twyman, James. (1998) *Emissary of Peace: A Vision of Light.*

Twyman, James. (2000) *The Secret of the Beloved Disciple.*

Twyman, James. (2000) *Portrait of the Master.*

Twyman, James. (2000) *Praying Peace: In Conversation with Gregg Braden and Doreen Virtue.*

Twyman, James. (2008) *The Moses Code: The Most Powerful Manifestation Tool in the History of the World.*

Twyman, James. (2009) *The Kabbalah Code: A True Adventure*.

Twyman, James. (2009) *The Proof: A 40-Day Program for Embodying Oneness*.

Vanzant, Iyanla. (2000) *Until Today*.

Vayro, Ian Ross. (2005) *They Lied To Us in Sunday School*.

Vayro, Ian Ross. (2007) *God Save Us From Religion*.

Vayro, Ian Ross. (2008) *Tears in Heaven*.

Virtue, Doreen. (1997) *The Lightworker's Way*.

Virtue, Doreen. (2006) *Divine Magic: The Seven Sacred Secrets of Manifestation* (book and CD).

Walker, Ethan III. (2003) *The Mystic Christ: The Light of Non-Duality and the Path of Love According to the Life and Teachings of Jesus*.

Walsch, Neale Donald. (1999) *Abundance and Right Livelihood: Applications for Living*.

Walsch, Neale Donald. (2000) *Bringers of The Light*.

Walsch, Neale Donald. (2002) *The New Revelations: A Conversation with God*.

Walters, J. Donald. (2000) *Awaken to Superconsciousness: How To Use Meditation for Inner Peace, Intuitive Guidance and Greater Awareness*.

Walters, J. Donald. (2000) *Meditations to Awaken Superconsciousness: Guided Meditations on The Light* (audio cassette).

Walters, J. Donald. (2003) *Meditation for Starters* (book and CD).

Walters, J. Donald. (2003) *Metaphysical Meditations* (audio CD).

Walters, J.Donald. (2003) *Secrets of Bringing Peace On Earth*.

Weisenthal, Simon. (1998) *The Sunflower: On the Possibilities and Limits of Forgiveness*.

Weiss, Brian. (2001) *Messages From the Masters: Tapping Into The Power of Love*.

Weiss, Brian. (2002) *Meditation: Achieving Inner Peace and Tranquility in Your Life* (book and CD).

Wilcock, David. *The Shift of the Ages – Convergence Volume One* (online book) [333]

Wilcock, David. *The Science of Oneness – Convergence Volume Two* (online book) [334]

Wilcock, David. *The Divine Cosmos – Convergence Volume Three* (online book) [335]

Wilcock, David. *Wanderer Awakening: The Life Story of David Wilcock* (online book) [336]

---

[333] http://divinecosmos.com/start-here/books-free-online/18-the-shift-of-the-ages
[334] http://divinecosmos.com/start-here/books-free-online/19-the-science-of-oneness
[335] http://divinecosmos.com/start-here/books-free-online/20-the-divine-cosmos
[336] http://divinecosmos.com/start-here/books-free-online/25-wander-awakening-the-life-story-of-david-wilcock

Wilcock, David. *The Reincarnation of Edgar Cayce* (online book) [337]

Wilcock, David. *The End of Our Century* (online book edited by David Wilcock) [338]

Wilcock, David. (2011) *The Source Field Investigations: The Hidden Science and Lost Civilizations Behind the 2012 Prophecies.*

Williamson, Marianne. (1996) *A Return To Love.*

Williamson, Marianne. (1997) *Morning and Evening Meditations and Prayers.*

Williamson, Marianne. (2002) *Everyday Grace: Having Hope, Finding Forgiveness and Making Miracles.*

Williamson, Marianne. (2003) *Being In Light* (audio CD set).

---

[337] http://divinecosmos.com/start-here/books-free-online/22-the-reincarnation-of-edgar-cayce-draft-of-pt-1
[338] http://divinecosmos.com/start-here/books-free-online/26-the-end-of-our-century

Wolf, Fred Alan. (1989). *Taking the Quantum Leap: The New Physics for Nonscientists*.

Wolf, Fred Alan. (2000). *Mind Into Matter: A New Alchemy of Science and Spirit*.

Wolf, Fred Alan. (2002). *Matter Into Feeling: A New Alchemy of Science and Spirit*.

Wolf, Fred Alan. (2004). *The Yoga of Time Travel: How the Mind Can Defeat Time*.

Wolf, Myke. (2010). *Create from Being: Guide to Conscious Creation*.

Yogananda, Paramahansa. (1979) *Metaphysical Meditations: Universal Prayers, Affirmations and Visualizations*.

Yogananda, Paramahansa. (2004) *The Second Coming of Christ: The Resurrection of the Christ Within You*.

Zukav, Gary. (1998) *The Seat of The Soul*.

Zukav, Gary. (2001) *Thoughts from The Seat of The Soul: Meditations for Souls in Process.*

Zukav, Gary and Francis, Linda. (2001) *The Heart of The Soul: Emotional Awareness.*

Zukav, Gary and Francis, Linda. (2003) *The Mind of The Soul: Responsible Choice.*

Zukav, Gary and Francis, Linda. (2003) *Self-Empowerment Journal: A Companion to The Mind of The Soul: Responsible Choice.*

Zukav, Gary. (2010) *Spiritual Partnership: The Journey to Authentic Power.*

About the Author

Michele Doucette is webmistress of Portals of Spirit, a spirituality website whereby one will find links to [1] The Enlightened Scribe, [2] an ezine called Gateway To The Soul, [3] books of spiritual resonance as well as authors of metaphysical importance, [4] categories of interest from Angels to Zen, [5] up-to-date information as shared by a Quantum Healer, [6] affiliate programs and resources of personal significance, [7] healing resource advertisements and [8] spiritual news.

As a Level 2 Reiki Practitioner, she sends long distance Reiki to those who make the request, claiming only to be a facilitator of the Universal energy, meaning that it is up to the individual(s) in question to use these energies in order to heal themselves.

Having also acquired a Crystal Healing Practitioner diploma (Stonebridge College in the UK), she is guardian to many from the mineral kingdom.

She is the author of several spiritual/metaphysical works; namely, [1] *The Ultimate Enlightenment For 2012: All We Need Is Ourselves*, a book that was nominated for the Allbooks Review Best Inspirational Book for 2011, [2] *Turn Off The TV: Turn On Your Mind*, [3] *Veracity At Its Best*, [4] *The Collective: Essays on Reality* (a composition of essays in relation to the Matrix), [5] *Sleepers Awaken: The Time Is Now To Consciously Create Your Own Reality*, [6] *Healing the Planet and Ourselves: How To Raise Your Vibration*, [7] *You Are Everything: Everything Is You*, [8] *The Awakening of Humanity: A Foremost Necessity*, [9] *The Cosmos of the Soul: A Spiritual Biography*, [10] *Getting Out Of Our Own Way: Love Is The Only Answer*, and [11] *Living The Jedi Way*, all of which have been published through St. Clair Publications.

In addition, she has written a separate volume that deals with crystals, aptly entitled *The Wisdom of Crystals*.

She is also the author of *A Travel in Time to Grand Pré*, a visionary metaphysical novel that historically ties the descendants of Yeshua (Jesus) to modern day Nova Scotia.

As shared by a reviewer, it is *Veracity At Its Best*, a spiritual (metaphysical) tome, that "constructs the context for the spiritual message" imparted in *A Travel in Time to Grand Pré*.

Against the backdrop of 1754 Acadie, it was the blending of French Acadian history with current DNA testing that contributed to the weaving of this alchemical tale of time travel, romance and intrigue.

From Henry I Sinclair to the Merovingians, from the Cathari treasure at Montségur to the Knights Templar, this novel, together with the words of Yeshua as spoken at the height of his ministry, has the potential to inspire others; for it is herein that we learn how individuals can find their way, their truth(s), so as to live their lives to the fullest.

Likewise, she has also published *Back Home with Evangeline*, the long awaited sequel to *A Travel in Time to Grand Pré*.

As is the case with all authors, she continues to read, research and write, when not teaching.

www.ingramcontent.com/pod-product-compliance
Lightning Source LLC
Chambersburg PA
CBHW061946070426
42450CB00007BA/1066